ABOUT THE AUTHOR

Cassandra Eason is a well-known author and broadcaster on psychic and spiritual experience, folklore and superstitions. She teaches different aspects of psychic development and is the author of several best-selling titles including *A Complete Guide to Magic and Ritual*, *A Complete Guide to Psychic Development*, *A Complete Guide to Divination*, *The Piatkus Guide to Pendulum Dowsing*, *The Piatkus Guide to Tarot* and *The Complete Book of Tarot*.

Aura
reading

Also by Cassandra Eason

Aura
reading

How to work with a
powerful healing energy

Cassandra Eason

PIATKUS

Copyright © 2000 by Cassandra Eason

Published in the UK in 2000 by
Judy Piatkus (Publishers) Ltd of
5 Windmill Street
London W1T 2JA
e-mail: info@piatkus.co.uk

Reprinted 2001 (twice)

The moral right of the author has been asserted

A catalogue record for this book is available from the British Library

ISBN 0 7499 2129 3

This book has been printed on paper manufactured with respect for the
environment using wood from managed sustainable resources

Set by Action Publishing Technology Ltd, Gloucester
Printed and bound in Great Britain by
Biddles Ltd, Guildford and King's Lynn
www.biddles.co.uk

CONTENTS

INTRODUCTION

Auras are energy fields that contain different colours and levels. They are seen spontaneously by clairvoyants, but, with practice, anyone can tune into and interpret auras.

Everything possesses an aura, even inanimate objects. Animate life forms possess a stronger aura because of the interactive energy flowing between themselves and the environment. There are, of course, considerable variations in what is regarded as animate life. The Native North Americans and other indigenous peoples would argue that stones and crystals are living and so essentially their auras change too – hence they can transmit healing energies.

For example, plants emit light round their forms that can be detected in Kirlian photography, a method of capturing auras on film (see Chapter 1). Plant auras fade when they are cut or deprived of water, but if a leaf is cut from a plant, the aura of the missing part remains on the Kirlian photograph.

Look at the Moon surrounded by its golden luminescence, or a beach with dancing mist through which the sun is breaking in tiny rainbows. People living in the country could forecast the weather from the Moon's aura, and though such phenomena can be explained in terms of atmospheric pressures, they are so much more. Recently I saw a huge fountain through which was arched a brilliant rainbow and around it the aura of misty water. This was a physical phenomenon, but on a deeper level it was truly mystical, for I felt I was in touch for the first time with the essence of water.

Some people do *see* auras externally and this is an ability that may evolve quite naturally as a result of working with auric fields. But even those with limited physical eyesight can become adept at seeing auras psychically. Auras are like butterflies. When we measure the wing span of a butterfly, analyse its composition and study its colours, we know but a small part of the butterfly's essential nature. The joy comes in observing its ethereal beauty, like a piece of paradise fluttering through the air.

Jesus, the Virgin Mary and many saints and holy men and women are depicted in paintings with golden haloes around their heads, and those who have met holy men and women describe either a golden or pink aura surrounding their whole bodies. A pink aura can also be clearly seen around the heads of mothers just after they have given birth – it is the merging of auras between mothers and children, fathers and children, husbands and wives or lovers that, at its best, results in close telepathic links.

The human aura is defined as the bio-energetic field surrounding the body. This field is believed to be created by the interaction of natural magnetic and electro-chemical reactions, combined with the energies of the subtle or spiritual forces within the body. Because this is not a static but an interactive energy, the aura that can be seen, felt or sensed reflects not only the essential person but their current emotional state, thoughts, desires and anxieties. The aura also forms an early warning system of potential problems and contains future opportunities that have not yet been manifest on the physical plane. Therefore aura reading is a powerful method of divination and especially clairvoyance. Because each aura is constantly interacting with other auras, it can also be affected by a particular environment, or the moods of those with whom the person comes into contact.

An individual aura forms the connecting point for the interchange of energies between people, animals and plants, and the Earth and cosmos. Since these energies can have a positive or negative, an energising or depleting effect, interpreting and strengthening one's own aura is important for increasing health and harmony, for protection against negativity, and for spiritual evolution. This spiritual/bio-energetic field varies in size and density under different conditions and is estimated to extend from between an inch to about three feet, approximately the extent of an extended arm. It surrounds the body as an ellipse. The Buddha's aura was said to extend and therefore influence people over a range of several miles.

Usually one or two colours predominate in the aura at a particular time, and one colour may endure over months or even years.

The process of *seeing* auras can be compared with the first time you visit an entirely new place. At first you experience a blur of sights, sound, fragrances and even tastes; nevertheless, you almost instantly gain an overall impression of the essential nature of the place. On subsequent visits you begin to identify specific landmarks, and after a number of visits to anticipate a particular house en route, the scent of a garden of tropical flowers, and even the first sounds of the sea; they are beyond the physical senses, but as you visualise them, they are evoked in your mind. So it is with auras – the first impression conveys the essential person and so will be of immense value, and gradually you will gain more detailed insight as you focus on specific levels.

CHILDREN AND AURAS

Young children will comment on the lovely blue light around the head of a grandmother who usually possesses evolved healing powers. They paint cows green and dogs yellow because they see the auric rather than the physical colour and become confused when told that their true colour is brown or black.

The auras of children are very clear and pure and they have

a radiance around them, unless they have been hurt badly or betrayed.

As we grow into the world of logic and formal learning, we forget how to see auras. So, as with many psychic arts, we have to relearn those abilities that were natural in childhood. This can involve simply relaxing into a state of openness and receptivity of childhood and trusting the evidence of the Inner Eye, which in children is not separated from the external. Imagination and visualisation are in adulthood, as in childhood, the entrance to the psychic world.

MY INTEREST IN AURAS

Not surprisingly, I encountered my first auras when I was researching children's psychic experiences. This began after my middle son, Jack, not quite three years old at the time told me that his father had fallen off his motorbike but was unhurt. Forty miles away, at that precise moment, the accident was happening. I discovered that many children also saw silvery lights surrounding them during out of body experiences; in one case a three-year-old girl described how a silvery form danced in front of her body as she walked down some steps.

As my research continued, I realised that the silvery mist of light that children frequently describe corresponded with clairvoyant accounts of the silver auric essence seen around the human form, one or two inches from the skin. A silver cord connecting the physical and etheric body is a feature which has been noted not only in cultures such as the Australian Aboriginal and Westernised spiritual movements such as Theosophy and Spiritualism, but has been witnessed by children and sensitive adults who knew nothing of such beliefs.

As a child, I had seen coloured lights around people and flowers, but as I grew older had dismissed these early experiences as imagination. After Jack's experience, I began to study psychic phenomena in both children and adults, and over the years realised I could sometimes detect and even anticipate people's moods by the colours around their heads. I saw these first as an inner picture, and then they seemed to actually surround the head of the person I was talking to.

But I began to doubt my abilities as I came into contact with the vast array of material and expectations proclaiming that auras were difficult. Then I found that I would see auras most clearly when I was tired and not trying to follow the designated steps to aura reading. For that reason my suggestions are only suggestions. You will soon, if you have not already, find by experiment the easiest and most effective way to work with auras.

Aura reading is not a separate spiritual art, but one strand in general psychic development, and is involved in divinatory and psychic arts you may already have tried. For example, psychometry, receiving psychic impressions by touch, is rooted in reading the aura of the object being held. In the case of stone or pottery from an ancient sacred site, its aura will contain events that have occurred at that place perhaps over the millennia, and the emotions experienced by those who lived and perhaps died there.

Magical rituals involve drawing cosmic and earth energies into the personal or collective aura – if a group is performing a spell – and transferring these to the symbol representing the wish or need. The coloured cone of power created in Wiccan ritual is one way of representing the cumulative auric energies of participants in a ritual.

Any form of psychic protection involves closing off the aura from negative outside influences to some degree. Healing, whether of yourself or loved ones, sends positive energies, usually described in terms of light, to strengthen and repair weaknesses in the auric energy field, and by using colours and crystals, stimulates the natural restorative energies of mind, body and soul.

This book offers basic information about the different

theories of the composition of the aura, its levels and colours. It also suggests methods of sensing and seeing the aura, both psychically and externally, ways of interpreting auras and of adapting the aura to specific situations or needs. Auric cleansing, balancing and strengthening and a variety of natural healing techniques are described, many of which use the natural world as a source of healing energy.

As you work through the book you will need a paint box or set of colouring pencils and paper, and a ring binder or loose leaf folder in which to record your auric impressions. You need no artistic skills, as you will only be recording colours round the shape of a head, a body or in concentric circles. You may find that the colours you record are very subtle at first, perhaps flashes of light or a soft grey or silver outline, but sometimes your subconscious will record much brighter shades, even though during the actual experience you were only aware of faint grey. In time you will be creating rainbow hues even in mundane situations.

The most important aspect is to practise seeing auras everywhere, in nature and the technological world alike – optic fibre lamps cast wonderful auras. Do not worry what is after-glow or artificial and what is *true* aura. In time your psyche will filter out the irrelevant material.

Chapter 1

THE HISTORY OF AURAS AND AURA READING

WHEN DID PEOPLE FIRST SEE AURAS?

It is likely that when our distant ancestors lived closer to the land an awareness of auras in both nature and people was universal. We can make this hypothesis because the ability survived among indigenous people until the technological world impinged upon their lives. For example, according to Native American wisdom, each herb and plant radiates a special aura, either a colour or an unmistakable essence. Medicine Men and Women, the Wise Ones, could identify from a missing or cloudy colour in the aura of a patient the corresponding herb that was needed to supplement the deficiency. Other members of the tribe also possessed this ability to harmonise auras and, on their initiatory Vision Quest, sometimes found a plant whose aura matched their own; this then became their power totem.

A 'vision quest' is a process of going out into nature, away from the distractions of everyday life, to create a sacred time and space, to be rather than do: to be silent rather than speak; to look with the inner eye and listen with the inner ear and move towards a new and often deeper level of one's spirituality.

It is a major rite of passage, akin to a naming ceremony, frequently practised among indigenous peoples at puberty. Although associated with the Native American Indians, this custom also features in Australian Aboriginal, Maori and

African cultures and is performed by other peoples who have close contact with the natural world. This rite, known by a myriad of different names, developed entirely independently in cultures separated by thousands of miles. Its purpose is that of healing, discovery, joy and a sense of connectedness with all things – four-legged and winged creatures, fish and insects, trees, stones, sky, stars and wind . . .

Over these few days of isolation the adolescent learns to draw power from nature into his or her own auric field, to see the interconnections of natural and human energies and to draw upon the healing and empowering biorhythms of nature for use in future times of need. The vision quest is also practised at any stage of life or age when there is a change-point or crisis, in order to renew auric and spiritual harmony with the natural world.

The earliest recorded auras are found in prehistoric Australian cave paintings that depict the creator/heroes with haloes. In Ancient Egypt the aura was shown both in tomb paintings and on papyri. In the Kabbalah, the Jewish system of esoteric wisdom, the world is said to be created by pure white light emanating or flowing from the godhead which divides and becomes the ten *sephiroth*, the 'splendid lights' or 'shining sapphires', each with different rainbow colours that are aspects of the divine and are contained in all life forms.

One of the earliest references to auras in European literature may be found in the writings of the medieval mystic Hildegard von Bingen. She was the first person to refer to *veriditas*, 'the greening principle', and she recounts her visions of luminous objects. Hindu sacred writings include many references to the 'thousand-petalled lotus of light' that surrounds the heads of those who have achieved enlightenment.

In Far Eastern cultures, treatment of illness through the aura dates back to time immemorial and is still widely practised. The chakras, psychic energy points in the body, are described as whirling petals of light and correspond to different colours. Through Theosophy, chakra theory has entered

Western consciousness as seven energy points that correspond with the seven levels or bodies that make up the aura.
In the 1970s these chakras became associated with the
colours of the rainbow that are seen in the human aura.

Western science began to study the human energy field
during the 1800s. In 1858 Baron Karl von Reichenbach
discovered emanations from plants, animals, people and
crystals, which he called the *odic* force.

RECORDING AURAS

The first visual images of the aura were created by Dr
William Kilner in 1911. He used different screens and dyes to
capture images of the aura on what became known as the
Kilner Screen, and he coined the term *aura*. He found that the
energy field varied from person to person and that it was
affected by the current physical condition of the subject
whose aura was being measured. As a result of his extensive
studies of human auras, Kilner developed a diagnostic system
based on the colour, texture, volume and appearance of the
energy field that was recorded on the screen.

The most famous recording device is Kirlian photography,
named after the Russian Semyon Kirlian, who discovered the
technique by accident in 1939. It is a method of high-
frequency electronic photography that reveals beautifully
patterned sparks and flares of energy emanating from living
creatures. Kirlian photography seems to be able to transfer
the aura of the subject to film by placing the subject of the
photograph, for example a leaf or a human hand, directly on
the film or photographic plate and passing high-frequency
electrical currents through it.

One of the most significant findings is that by studying
aura photographs of the fingers, palms and feet, disorders in
the auric body are revealed before any symptoms are manifest in the physical body. For example, the aura ring around
each finger of a healthy person is circular and complete;

broken aura rings indicate incipient problems in the body. The palms and feet of people who are well appear quite clear. However, on the aura photographs, black spots in the auras of these parts of the body are a warning of more general energy blockages that, if untreated, will develop into physical problems.

Experiments in February 1988 at the Neuropsychiatric Institute at UCLA in California showed energy flares emanating from the fingertips of healers. Research has further determined that this energy is concentrated in hundreds of points on the body that seem to correspond to Chinese acupuncture points.

Dr Valerie Hunt at UCLA also conducted detailed experiments in which a clairvoyant-healer, the Reverend Rosalyn Bruyere of the Healing Light Center in Glendale, California, described the colour, size and energy movements of the chakras and auras of a healer and patient. The results showed that mathematical energy patterns of healer and patient corresponded to the auric colours observed by the psychic. The experiment was successfully replicated with seven different aura readers.

Dr Hunt commented: 'Throughout the centuries in which sensitives have seen and described the auric emissions, this is the first objective electronic evidence of frequency, amplitude and time, which validates their subjective observation of colour discharge.'

Recent research into the auras of plants and humans has found that the electromagnetic fields of living organisms interact with and affect one another, far beyond the physical confines of the body. By hooking plants up to electronic equipment, researchers discovered that plants respond intensely to the thoughts of people in their environment. The death or threat of death to living cells, whether human, plant or animal, caused intense electromagnetic reactions in plants that were not personally threatened.

One plant energy researcher, Marcel Vogel, experimented

with children and plants, instructing the children to move their hands backwards and forwards gently over the leaves. Eventually, the plants began to sway with the movement of the child's hand, although there was no physical contact between the child and the plant, and no breeze.

There are several theoretical models of the aura which describe a human aura in terms of several layers or bodies that interpenetrate and surround each other in successive layers. In these models, each body in turn is more ethereal and vibrates at a higher frequency than the body that it encloses, so that the outermost layer is often seen as purple, which has the highest colour vibrations in the spectrum and is the most ethereal. The most frequently expressed theory of auras hypothesises seven levels. Thus, the outermost layer is linked to cosmic forces and contains the seeds of possibilities. Specific colours are associated with each level.

AURIC BODIES

Terminology can be very confusing and when you read of different levels of aura or auric bodies, these are not a series of separate bodies within the physical form, but a basic spirit body that may be the part of us that survives death. The auric layers are perceived as radiating from the superimposed spiritual body, so on one level the etheric self is very close to the physical form. But it is also connected to the cosmos, and the more spiritually evolved we become the more significant these cosmic layers are in our everyday world, and the easier it is to make the transition from physical to eternal life.

If you study the aura of a flower that has been newly picked and is in water, the aura will be bright. Continue to study the aura each day and you may notice that even after a short while, the aura becomes paler. As the petals fade and the leaves become brown, you will see the aura diminishing. This is why some people do not like cut flowers, but prefer to keep only plants that are growing in soil in their homes.

When the flower is dead, the aura will be gone. So what happens to the light?

When a person dies or is dying, circles of light are seen around the body. These *corpse candles,* as they have been called over the centuries, are said to be the soul leaving a body after death. Through the ages relatives of a dying person have reported seeing a series of lights floating towards that person. These are believed to be the essences of departed relatives coming to welcome the newly deceased person. From my extensive research into this subject, and from witnessing the phenomenon at my own mother's death, I have found that, as a person dies, those watching will comment that the whole face is suffused with golden light and the dying person looks momentarily young and well again. Then, sometimes with the sound of the voice fading away as though down a long tunnel, the light fades from the face and may be perceived as a light hovering in the room, which then disappears upwards. There are countless testimonies to all or part of this *dying in the light,* reported in different ages and parts of the world.

Lights are also seen by women at the time, or in the days or weeks before, a child is conceived, and some interpret this as the etheric or spirit body of the child seeking a new life form with a chosen family. Ancient traditions tell how we all came from a particular star and that our astral twin self waits there during our period on earth. After death, our etheric body is said to rejoin its other more perfected half, once it has learned the necessary lessons and made the earth a better place.

Evidence from the study of near-death experiences throughout the world suggests that people can exist independently of the physical body in an astral or spirit body. Out of body experiences offer similar proof. The body of an astral traveller, viewed from above by the traveller and by those who observe the phenomenon, appears almost lifeless – *empty,* as someone described to me when she discovered her brother having an out of body experience.

Gilbert Attard, a French psychic researcher with a special interest in physics and magnetic energies, sees this auric energy as explaining apparitions that are seen by many people at the same time:

> Each of us can emit an 'aura' which is one of the fundamentals of the visible spectrum. Several people together will emit the sum of the frequency which is a white light, the sum of the three fundamental colours, blue, red and yellow. The point of impact of the white light will be the convergence point of all the human eyes. What is interesting in this natural physical phenomenon is that it can explain some of the phenomena called supernatural, for example the apparitions of the Virgin Mary and the white light that is often mentioned around her. In effect, several individuals focus their attention on a particular point in space to create a virtual image. If my theory is correct, it raises a question: what provokes this phenomenon? Is it the combination of different energies coming from the ground (magnetic fields, static charges, etc.)?
>
> Are certain places, such as Lourdes and San Diamiano, more propitious than others?
>
> There may be a new possibility which combines perfectly the two preceding ideas. Is there an intelligence outside of our own which knows this physical principle and can use it to communicate with us by using mental power to project holographic images? In such a case are we dealing with extraterrestrial beings?

Gilbert's theory may seem revolutionary but it recognises the complex interaction between the physical and psychic aspects of the aura and deserves considerably more investigation.

Exercise: Detecting the auras of inanimate objects

In the Introduction I mentioned that psychometry was associated with auras, because the aura of even a seemingly inanimate object can absorb auric impressions from present or

*previous owners of a house or site with which they are associ-
ated. Psychometry has been described as the etheric or soul's
eye. In the following exercise, you will not make direct contact
with an artefact itself, but with its aura.*

*Go to a museum or reconstructed industrial area in which
authentic items have been collected and are in the hands-on
section – a good time to choose is early morning or late in the
afternoon when it is quiet.*

- *Walk around until you find an artefact to which you are
  attracted. I first tried this in a museum in Winchester,
  Hampshire, where pieces of Roman pottery could be
  handled. Broken objects are especially fascinating to work
  with as you can often trace the missing outline at auric level.*

- *Hold your hands apart and gently begin to circle them,
  curving your fingers as though holding the object above the
  object, moving closer until you encounter the outer limits
  of the aura. You will feel this as resistance and slight pressure a few centimetres from the object, like an invisible
  membrane.*

- *When you feel this slight pressure, move your hands in
  circles over the aura itself and you may feel a slight tingle
  or warmth.*

- *Close your eyes as you work and allow impressions to
  form. Whether an aura belongs to a human, a plant or artefact, you are not just registering a colour or colours, but
  the impressions the hopes, fears and joys contained within
  the auric field.*

- *You may see in your mind's eye a predominant
  colour/colours, or perhaps hear sounds, smell fragrances.
  From these may form images of people and places.*

- *When you feel the connection ceasing, take your hands
  away carefully to avoid disturbing these impressions and
  either write or sketch your findings. Once more, colour in
  your images.*

- *Over the weeks, whenever you go to an historic site or even
  a modern home, continue to read the auras of objects.*

Chapter 2

HOW TO SEE AURAS

Most people are able to sense or see auras to some degree, whether as one large field with a predominant hue and patterns or multiple fields of colour.

Exercise: Seeing auras in nature

The best way to become aware of auras is by observing those in the natural world. Animals and birds are totally unselfconscious and therefore do not mask their auras. Moving auras are perhaps the easiest to register. Birds are the best focus of all as you can see a collective aura around a flock created by the accumulated energy of harmonised flight.

- *Wait until it is starting to get dusk on a clear day so there is a pale grey background.*
- *Find a place, for example trees near a clearing, a dovecote or cliff-face where birds fly around in the evening. A rookery is ideal as rooks make a final swirl each night.*
- *Half close your eyes, letting the scene absorb you – the sounds, the fragrances – and look not at the birds but at the shapes they are making as they fly.*
- *Allow your eyes to go into soft focus by looking slightly to the side and beyond the swirling mass, so that the birds are on the outer ranges of your vision.*
- *The key to good aura reading is empathy, so allow your imagination to make you one of the birds and feel the crisp air and the sensation of flying.*
- *If you can, begin watching birds sitting on top of the dove-*

cote or along wires and then observe the increasing momentum as they fly off. This allows the auric picture to build up.

- Each bird will exude light, perhaps following its natural outline, that you may perceive initially as pale grey or silver luminescence. The aura will deepen as the bird moves, like gentle waves tinged by silver. However, you may perceive almost from the first a silvery blue, the special aura of creatures of the sky. Look only for a minute or two or until you feel you are having to make an effort or doubts are intruding.

Exercise: The aura of stillness

The next stage is to observe an aura when a person is still, although the aura is moving gently as it interacts with the world around it.

- Again, use soft late afternoon or early evening light as a backdrop. If you have a cat, it is the perfect subject while at rest or concentrating, and if the cat is aware of your watching, auric colours of love, pink and green may enter its sphere. You may even detect purple if you have a very wise cat. Alternatively, use a tree or a large brilliant flower. Sunflowers and roses are especially good subjects as they have, over the centuries, accumulated so many legends and positive feelings from people that they carry powerful innate auric vibes.

- Sit where you are comfortable and can look slightly beyond and to the side of the subject, so that it is in soft focus. As before, empathise, whether with animal, tree or flower, so you are aware of texture – visualise the sensation of rough bark or soft, fragrant petals against your skin. Aura reading is a multi-sensory process.

- Animals who are loved naturally have a pink aura, plus the brown of the earth, especially if they spend time outdoors. If they are healthy, this will be a rich golden brown, like a ploughed field in the noonday sun. The flower may have an *aura that mirrors its colour, but paler and, like a tree, exude green and rich brown, merging to blue or silver where it is framed against the sky. It is no accident that the elemental colours of Earth and Water, green and blue, mirror the colours of the aura of Nature herself.*

- *Be patient if you see pale grey or silvery auras at first. The full colour vision of childhood will return if you do not force it.*

- *If you see the auras of birds, animals or plants, paint or colour your impressions immediately afterwards. Concentrate on the colours. Van Gogh, for example, painted the auras of what he saw, the forms were secondary. Allow your hands to select colours without conscious choice.*

- *Keep these pictures and study the same subjects at different times, for example birds just before a storm or when disturbed by predators, and plants at different seasons and in different weather.*

SEEING INDIVIDUAL AURAS

The auric field will vary in size and density under different conditions and from individual to individual. Though the aura extends all around the body in a sphere, it is most easily seen around the head, so initially this is the best place to look for other people's auras. However, studying the aura around your hands, especially the palms, is the most effective way to observe your own aura easily without using a mirror.

Clairvoyance means *clear seeing*, the psychic vision of the Third or Inner Eye that tradition states is situated at brow level, slightly above and between the physical eyes. This is a major chakra or psychic energy point (see Chapter 6).

Experiment with different methods until you find the one that seems right for you.

In the exercises above, you used visualisation as a key method of tuning into auras in the natural world and those surrounding inanimate objects. All psychic experience begins through *imaging*, to which the word *imagination* is related. We access our psychic powers through the imagination and one day, like driving a car, you find the process has imperceptibly become automatic.

Begin by visualising a really spectacular collective aura, and then focus on individual ones within the scene.

Aura visualisation

Visit a traditional fairground or a theme park with music playing and many children playing and rushing around enjoying themselves. A multi-coloured context will add to the brilliance so choose a brightly decorated setting on a sunny day with flowers blooming and trees in blossom. Alternatively, visit the scene at night when there are many coloured lights and perhaps a fireworks display. The colour, sounds, smells, and above all the constant movement of excited children will create swirling bands of colour.

Focus directly on the overall impression of the colours and allow the sounds and fragrances to enter you and become part of you. Let the colours swell and rise to form a huge rainbow arch overhead.

Now choose one particularly happy child and imagine you are a child once more, seeing the brilliance through his or her eyes, dashing around gathering sounds and colour in a huge rainbow bubble that expands and then bursts into brilliant beams of light. Focus on the child, close your eyes, blink and look at the child through half-closed eyes, only now casting your vision slightly out of focus so that the colours merge.

Next, open your eyes wide, look above the head of the child and visualise a halo of colours. Continue until you actually *see* the colours, either in your mind's eye without effort or externally. Do not worry about recording the colours, but keep transferring your gaze to the collective auric rainbow in the sky then to different children, to young lovers in a pink haze, to a baby asleep with a gentle golden halo of purity above him or her. In each case visualise the vision and hold it until you can see it. It you find a reflective surface, look for your own rainbow above your head. Then concentrate on enjoying yourself, and by the end of the day you will find it hard to stop seeing rainbows.

The following exercise is designed to help you sense and see auras under controlled situations. In time, you will automatically see auras, even in broad daylight or under harsh lighting, especially the first predominant auric impression.

Some people, myself included, automatically tense when told they are going to perform an exercise to make something happen. Anxiety can inhibit natural clairvoyance, so if you do feel that your intuitions are not flowing, recall the spontaneity of those fairground rainbows and continue to rely on visualisation to kick-start your natural ability to perceive your own aura or that of the person for whom you are reading.

Exercise: Sensing the auric field

Touch is an easy way to tune into and interpret auras. There are several variations of this method; the following is one way to try it.

- *Hold your hands about 15cm apart, fingers spread wide, palms facing each other. Close your eyes.*

- *Slowly bring your hands together until they touch. Repeat this sequence two or three times.*

- *Most people, when they do this exercise for the first time, describe a warmth and heaviness around the hands as they bring their hands close together. The sensation has been likened to trying to bring the same poles of two magnets together – the closer they get, the more they repel each other.*

- *Once you have experienced this sensation, hold your hands in the original position, again about 15cm away.*

- *Now bring your hands together so that they nearly touch, move them apart, move them back together.*

- *Continue this for five or six cycles.*
- *You may feel the auric field building up like a wall of energy. If you do not feel anything, repeat the exercise, but this time* imagine *the sensation and each day carry out the exercise purely as a visualisation until the actual sensations kick in. Try it when you are sleepy and relaxed.*

Different schools of thought exist as to whether you should study auras against a dark or light background. When you first begin, you may see a grey or silvery outline, the first and innermost auric level of the etheric body that is visible about three centimetres beyond and following the outline of the physical body. For this, a light background is obviously best. However, while you do not want total darkness, a more muted setting may help you to see or project colours – either against twilight or early morning light, perhaps in a room lit by gentle candlelight.

Previously I have mentioned allowing your eyes to go into soft focus or even out of focus. The reason is that ethereal substances such as ghosts are frequently perceived out of the corner of one's eye, and the focused area of vision is inevitably limited. If you have ever been aware of a shadowy form or movement right on the edge of your field of physical vision, you may in fact have seen an aura or an etheric body, perhaps that of a friend or lover who was thinking of you strongly at that moment – such living ghosts are well attested in my own psychic research. A similar phenomenon can occur when you are lying in bed in the early morning, or late at night, looking through half-closed misted eyes at the world. Some researchers believe that your psychic vision increases at times when physical sight is at its least focused.

Exercise: Observing your own field

- *Hold your hands against a dark background with the fingers and palms almost touching each other. Then move them apart quickly. You may see bands of greyish light* extend from the fingers of one hand to the other.

- *If you lower one hand about 15cm below the other, you may see diagonal rays connecting the fingers.*

- *If you see nothing either externally or in your mind's vision, try again another day, if necessary beginning with visualisation.*

- *Next, either by candlelight or perhaps natural twilight, hold your hands in front of your face, palms facing away from you at a distance of about 60cm. The space between your fingertips should be about 5cm. If possible, use a plain white wall for a background.*

- *If you let your eyes relax you may see a silvery grey glow following the shape of your hands – the auric energy from your etheric body. This is sometimes described as pale smoke clinging to the skin.*

- *If you try this several times over a period of days you may become aware of a narrow band of colours and/or sparks flaring beyond the silvery grey. This auric energy was present from the beginning of your explorations, but like seeing in the dark, your psychic vision is adapting and will continue to become clearer and more differentiated over the weeks and months. If you persist, the band of colour may expand to a thick vibrant strip, several inches wide. You may also notice that the brightness and colour varies according to your mood and state of health.*

- *Music is a particularly evocative stimulus. Experiment with different types – classical, jazz or pop – and record your findings.*

- *As you begin to see colours, paint or colour an image of your hands and then look at the aura around your feet, another clear area, and finally look in a mirror at the aura around your head.*

AURA READING FOR OTHERS

Work with a person with whom you feel totally relaxed and who you know will not criticise or cast doubt on your abilities. The adult aura is more complex and less clearly defined than that of children so this exercise will take time and patience.

Ask your subject to lie down or sit in a chair with their palms uppermost. Beginning with the head of the subject, gently pass your hands down each side of the body, palms down, and fingers curved as though you were holding something very delicate, about 6cm (2–3in) from the body, paying special attention to the palms and the feet, until you feel resistance.

As with the psychometric exercise, follow the line of the invisible membrane, which may dip in a wavy line or almost disappear in places if a person is tired or anxious. In humans this firm resistance a few centimetres from the body, following the outline of the body, is marking out the etheric aura.

Now move outwards a few centimetres at a time and see if you can trace an oval-shaped invisible membrane. Continue to move your fingers outwards, tracing successive layers that will become less dense the further you move from the body. As you move through the aura, you may feel a tingling sensation, like a mild electrical charge, warmth, vibrations and perhaps swirls of sudden energy or even knots.

Move gently and sensitively, and feel through your fingertips rather than seeing through your eyes. Eventually, when you feel nothing more, you have reached the outer limits of the aura. Do not be surprised if you see flashes of light or colours flowing down the arms or even legs. This is natural auric energy.

Close your eyes and see in your mind's vision one or two predominant colours. Alternatively, close your eyes, open them, and focus not directly at the head of the subject but at the space around the head and shoulders, and allow one or two major colours to form as a haze.

Do not try to analyse colour meanings, but allow spontaneous impressions of the emotions and potentialities contained in them to form.

Developing aura observation in the everyday world

In the early stages, concentrate on picking up the predominant colour or colours of people you observe. It is easiest to perceive a subject's aura if he or she is thinking or communicating on a subject they feel very passionate about. Go and listen to speakers at meetings or lectures, or observe a friend talking about his or her new lover, or a new mother with her baby. If working outdoors, stand so that the sun is behind you and create a backdrop from clouds or trees, remembering that these also exude auras. Allow your eyes to relax and go into early morning waking mode, then look above and behind the person until you detect the auric glow, gradually moving your gaze closer to the head and form.

Continue to watch people in a variety of situations. The importance at this stage is observing rather than analysing auras, and your intuitive impressions will be your best guide. For this reason it is better to concentrate on perceiving auras before interpreting them. However, if you do want to refer to colour meaning, see Chapter 3.

Your initial impressions will usually be confirmed by the specific colour interpretations and may run counter to verbal and non-verbal signals. For example, the politician talking about saving the environment may be registering not Mother Earth colours of green or rich browns, but yellow for avarice, a harsh blue reflecting a desire for power above everything, or a dirty yellow that may reveal less than honest intent.

Become aware of how the predominant colour/s of an aura can change very rapidly. Again, you can use colour correspondences to analyse the significance of changing auric shades, but what is especially significant is how an aura can become clouded or suddenly brilliant and perhaps exude sparks or flashes of colour. To observe colour changes, a subdued background is best, either pale natural northern light or candlelight.

REGISTERING CHANGES IN THE AURA

Once more, use a friend or family member, someone who will not become upset when exploring feelings, as this is quite a personal, intense form of exploration. It begins and ends on a positive note, but you could also burn lavender or rose oil for love and emotional harmony in the room in which you are working.

Look at the subject while he or she is totally relaxed in a comfortable but well-supported chair that does not hide their outline. Alternatively, the subject can lie on a bed or couch face upwards, wearing fairly close-fitting clothes.

Begin by asking the person to recall a time when he or she experienced intense love, perhaps the first time of falling in love, the consummation of the relationship or some other moment of great joy or triumph. Ask the subject to visualise the event in detail, recalling the words and setting.

Sit quietly and throw your eyes slightly out of focus. If you find this difficult, one easy method is to concentrate on a point six or nine inches beyond the subject so that the subject is only vaguely discernible but the general outline can be seen. Once more, the area of the head is a source of stronger overall impressions, but you may detect a radiance around the whole body, with more intense colours around the head, hands and feet. Begin with your overall impression of the predominant colours and the intensity of the hue. Note any flashes, flares or sparks. Quickly paint or colour what you see.

Next ask the person to remember a time when he or she was very angry or sad. Once more, ask the subject to recreate in their mind the associated sounds and sensations. Scribble down the colours/auric impressions you see and then tell the subject to allow the negative feelings to ebb away and see how the aura becomes paler and less intense.

It is important to end a session by replacing negativity with positive feelings. Direct the subject to visualise a time and place when he or she was totally at peace, tranquil and in harmony either with the self, another person or a place. This time ask the person to describe the scene, and as well as observing gentler, more subtle hues, you may see swirls of energy moving towards you. Try to illustrate this. Afterwards, spend some time showing the subject the colours you captured and talk quietly, perhaps sharing a simple meal or listening to music.

I have already mentioned the Third Eye as the symbolic source of clairvoyant vision. The following exercise is one that if practised once a month will help to develop and strengthen your clairvoyant powers. You will need a large oval mirror in which you can see at least the top half of your body.

Exercise: Strengthening your clairvoyant vision

- *Arrange a semi-circle of small amethysts in front of the mirror so that when you light candles they will reflect the light. Purple glass nuggets are a good substitute.*

- *Wait until early evening and light a horseshoe of indigo or deep purple candles, the colour associated with the brow chakra, at a safe distance behind you, so that the light is reflected as a gentle glow within the mirror.*

- *Using either a deep purple face paint or burgundy eyeshadow or lipstick, draw the Eye of Horus, an Ancient Egyptian hieroglyphic that has been used throughout the world in many ages as a talisman of protection and also a symbol of clairvoyance, in the centre of your brow, between and slightly above your eyes.*

- *In the mirror, focus on the Third Eye and the area around it and before long you should see a silver mist emanating from it that surrounds the outline of your head and upper body. Follow the outline for a few centimetres away from the skin.*

- *Return your gaze to the Third Eye and soon colours will form and circle the body in a moving, swirling ellipse a few more centimetres from the silver outline.*

- *If you sway slightly you will see the colours move correspondingly, and before long the aura of the crystals and candles will be visible and will make your own aura richer and deeper.*

- *Gradually let the colours fade and sit in the glow of the candles, allowing auric impressions to ebb and flow, as they will.*

- *Turning round, extinguish the candles one by one, sending the light to whoever needs it, not forgetting yourself.*

- *Collect together the amethysts and place them by your bed while you sleep, for gentle clairvoyant visions and swirling colours will strengthen your aura so you awake refreshed.*

BREAKING DOWN THE BARRIERS TO AURIC VISION

Before the onslaught of the technological world indigenous peoples did not need to practise seeing or interpreting auras. As the wise ones shared the legends of the birds, the flowers, and the trees, the weather and the changing seasons, the essence of nature became personified, and colours were absorbed as rainbow beams when a sudden shower fell on a field of sunflowers, when dew sparkled on the dawn grass or snow melted to reveal the first flowers of spring.

So whether you intend to practise aura interpretation for professional counselling or healing purposes or as a personal way of keeping in touch with your own deeper feelings and those of your family and friends, the natural world is as it has always been; a gateway to developing the instinctive awareness of joys, sorrows and dreams as they are mirrored in the spectrum of the human biofield.

Right now might not be a good time for you to get away from work or home commitments and go off to spend a week quietly in the natural world. However, if you do get the chance to have a mini-vision quest over the next few weeks – perhaps a day or an overnight stay in the countryside – then your awareness of the energy fields of those around you, human and animal, will increase quite spontaneously.

In the modern world where you can experience the thrill of riding on the back of a dinosaur from the comfort of a cinema seat, why walk in the woods where you will only see squirrels or rabbits and then only after an hour or more sitting in silence? Over time, in a crowded workplace or urban street, the natural flow of auric energies between people and the natural world, as well as between each other, gets dulled. This effect is mirrored in human interactions, so we can no longer so readily tune in to the auras around those we meet, one of the truly wondrous and yet quite normal abilities buried within us.

The vision quest

Ideally, a vision quest lasts up to seven days; two or three days of preparation; two in solitude and one afterwards to share the insights with companions or, if you are alone, to record them. The length is less important than the experience, because vision quests are essentially internal journeys of the soul. You can join an organized group (though some of the formal vision quests can be physically gruelling and thus counterproductive) or you can pitch a tent or trailer for a long weekend at a local nature reserve or Forestry Commission site. You do not need mountainous or remote countryside – you can even have your vision quest in your own garden. If you undertake a one day vision quest, you can spend the morning in preparation, the afternoon communing with nature and the evening gathering together the meaning of what you have seen.

If you are new to psychic work or have become disillusioned with the often contradictory and increasingly technical approach to what is essentially personal intuitive exploration into the soul, time in the natural world will not only open you to a variety of auric impressions, but regenerate your aura's natural protective and self-healing powers – enhancing the forgotten ability of childhood to see into the heart of life in glorious Technicolor.

If you go with friends, you can each retire to a separate tent or place to carry out your individual quests, coming together for the preparation and sharing insights afterwards.

Preparation:

In the few days before you go practise withdrawing for a few moments when you are alone in a natural setting. Let your surroundings fade as you breathe in through your nose and out, steadily and quietly, through your mouth.

Close your eyes, open them, blink and you will find that one specific object has come prominently into focus and blots all others from consciousness. It may be a flower, a leaf or a piece of wood on the ground. Let it speak to you in your mind's ear and understand how its essential strength can find an echo within you.

Let an aura form quite naturally around the object. If you continue to watch, without effort you will see that the energies around even a flower do have subtle variations. You began to study this with Aura of Stillness on (page 10). In fact they may seem to move towards you and mingle with the light that appears to come from you when you are still. If you are not aware of the interaction, do not force the impression, just send positive feelings towards your focus.

The night before your quest:

On the night before your quest (or in the late morning of a single day quest), light a small fire and burn sage for wisdom, cedar or sandalwood for purification and finally dried lavender for blessings and protection. Let the smoke aura cleanse you of doubts and fill you with a sense of harmony.

When you arrive:

You should spend the first day or hours (depending on how long you have) letting the pressures of life slip from you. Eat simple, natural foods that will allow your digestion to relax; seeds; pasta or rice, fruits and vegetables, lean chicken or fish. Cut out caffeine and alcohol but do not attempt to fast.

Increase your periods of letting the world slip away by focusing on a single blade of grass or flower and allowing it to move out of focus. As you become more experienced, you will not need to close your eyes and open them, but will find that an object will naturally come to the fore of your vision.

Gradually you will be aware, if you continue to send positive thoughts, that you are experiencing a momentary sense of becoming the grass blown by the wind or the flower unfolding in the sunshine. It is quite a moving experience and through this channel you may start to understand things about yourself and the world. You do not need to time these periods as you will find that time naturally expands as you move deeper into yourself.

Preparing your site:

During the day (or morning if it is a mini-quest) you should begin to gather the tools you will need for your quest and four symbols (a feather, a clear quartz, a shell and a rounded black or brown stone) to represent the major elemental energies that will mark out the main directions of your circle.

- *Use a compass to find North and try to align your vision place so that you are facing the East or rising sun.*
- *As you find or unpack each object see and connect with its aura.*
- *Place the feather in the East for the power of Air to connect you with the wisdom of the winds and to the aura of the feather (as it is now and as it was as part of aura of the bird flying through the sky). Send positive thoughts to it and let them return to strengthen your auric field. You may feel your own biofield getting lighter as it is suffused with the excitement of soaring through the sky.*
- *Use the clear quartz for the element of Fire and the noon sun in the South. A shining white stone will serve as well. Connect with your quartz by placing it in front of you and see the shimmering aura of frozen light. You may feel your own energy field become brighter and warmer because of the connection.*
- *Place the shell in the West for the power of the ocean and waters of the earth. Let its aura, effervescent like sea or cascading water-falls, flow into and energise your own auric field.*
- *Finally, in the North, place the rounded black or brown stone, from the area where you are staying, to connect you to the power and protection of the earth. Though dark, the stone may have a golden aura, like a newly ploughed field. Let it make you feel safe and protected and you may feel the surge of auric energy beneath your feet.*

Constructing your circle:

Next you need to construct the circle, which should be large enough to sit comfortably or lie in. Prepare your circle in a sheltered spot, perhaps near the entrance to your tent or under trees in your garden.

- *Cut a pliable branch (any fruit or nut-bearing tree will serve as a symbol of fertility).*
- *Bind the branch into a sacred hoop to represent the circle of the seasons and the natural world. Alternatively create a circle of stones.*

- *Place a colourful blanket or rag rug made of natural fibres underneath it.*
- *You will also need a blanket or sleeping bag to cover yourself if it is cool or when you doze.*

Your vision quest:

Some traditionalists begin a vision quest at dusk, but it seems more natural to begin refreshed and for any natural anxieties to run through your mind in the daylight, so that you are free by the evening to let visions come. Eat a light meal the night before and go to bed early after a shower or swim in a lake or sea to remove all your past angers, resentments and regrets.

Many formal modern vision quests fail because physical deprivations, commonplace to tribesmen, are so much of a shock to modern men and women that unrealistic expectations create a sense of failure that can run counter to what should be a spiritual experience. Native peoples were brought up to experience days of hardship in the open air, but in the modern world few of us could sit out day and night, perhaps in rain or cold without ill effects. Eat light natural food, filled with the life force or *prana* – nuts, seeds, fruit, bread and cheese – at regular intervals. Drink mineral water and if it rains too hard, retire inside your tent with the flap open.

- *Begin at dawn (or noon if you are doing a day quest). Enter the circle after drinking pure mineral water and face each of the directions in turn, beginning with the South.*
- *Hold each of your four symbols of power from the four directions, feeling their natural forces entering and washing over you. Their auric fields will form a circle round your own aura, strengthening it and cleansing it of all that is not positive, so you may experience the ebb and flow of a range of emotions. If at any time during your quest you lack inspiration, hold your symbols*

again to connect with nature and source in your mind's eye, soaring high with the bird, carried by the east wind, warmed by the sunny south, riding the crest of the wave in the west and seeing the ancient stone circles in the north.

- *Do not consciously strive to sleep or stay awake. If you can spend more than one day on your quest, your body will fall into a natural rhythm as you wake and sleep with the sun, although your sleep will be more of half-dreams in which your deepest insights may come.*

- *Allow worries and daily concerns to pass through your mind, but do not consciously try to solve them or anticipate the future.*

- *At regular intervals, fix on a blade of grass as before, but let it move out of focus and close your eyes as you wish. The colours around you may change as different natural auras blend, assume eminence and fade into the background. You may see yourself first encircled in green swirls of light, then framed in the gold of the sun, then the silver of moonlight. This is true aura contact and is what all the complex techniques devised by modern gurus are trying to express.*

- *You may want to sit or lie or change your position. Follow your natural feelings and when you need a drink or to relieve yourself, do so with minimum contact with others, apart from a friendly smile and greeting.*

- *You may find that certain sounds, like bird song or rain, seem to fill your being. Colours will become more vivid, cold and heat more intense and a specific animal, bird, rock or plant will have a message for you or give you his or her strength. Its aura is momentarily yours and on an unconscious level you also are passing your insights to it.*

- *The past may return, old voices, images, old sorrows. Do not resist, but as they pass see them carried away on the wind – your aura is being stripped of what is no longer of use, like autumn leaves blowing from a branch.*

- *Accept whatever messages you are given and do not try to incorporate them into the everyday world. It is not yet time to return.*

- *When dawn breaks for the second or third time if you are able to carry out a full quest or at an appropriate natural change-point* for a shorter quest, perhaps a thunderstorm or the piercing call of an owl, your experience will end. You will know when the time is right.

After your quest:

Following a shower and a light, cooked meal you are ready perhaps to sleep for a while or to share your new insights with friends who may also have been undertaking their own quests. If you are alone, write, draw, paint the auras you saw or even sing your new understanding of yourself and your relationship with the universe.

You may need to undertake vision quests two or three times a year, to remove any new blockages and traumas and expand your new understanding as your life unfolds and to reactivate your auric awareness if life has clouded it. In time you will find that even an hour in the park will allow you to absorb power from the natural world and that as a result you are refreshed, relaxed and cleansed of all your auric garbage.

Chapter 3

AURAS AND COLOURS

We talk about *feeling blue, being in a black mood* or *green with envy.* These terms refer to the auras cast by these particular states of mind. Colours represent the different vibrational levels in the auric field and each is interpreted according to traditional colour meanings. These meanings have partly been created by observing certain auras that are associated with particular qualities. For example, great and noble leaders may display a strong blue aura that becomes purple when the leader is expressing wisdom or altruism; these colours have thus become linked with leadership and true nobility of spirit.

Each colour has positive or negative connotations according to its shade and clarity. For example, a predominantly red aura can indicate either anger or courage. The interpretation of intent, however, goes beyond the actual shades perceived and involves the intuitive processes used to decide whether a Tarot card or rune is displaying its positive or challenging aspect – this sensitivity comes as you read and interpret auras.

Though physical conditions can be revealed in a colour change, especially if there is an emotional or spiritual cause of dis-ease, they are also manifest as dark spots, tears or holes in the aura (see Chapter 8).

We all possess a complete rainbow within our auras. But, even when you can see all the subtleties of colour in the different levels, one particular aura is usually prominent. Under normal circumstances, when our emotions are balanced, our personal permanent auric colour shines through. For example, if you are a loving person or are concerned with environmental issues and live close to nature, your aura will be manifest as green, because green is the colour associated with Mother Nature. The other colours are still present and can be observed, but the green radiates most strongly.

However, throughout the day, situations and people may temporarily affect your auric colour, for example if you are concentrating on learning something new, streaks or even bands of yellow, already present in the aura, would become more prominent; if you were working on your spiritual development, the purple area of your aura would become evident.

As thoughts, feelings, and desires permeate the stable auric colour, colour variations may manifest themselves as streaks. However, the mood colour may temporarily override the permanent hue, if the emotion is strong.

If an event is very significant, for example falling in or out of love, permanent colour can change. A person whose predominant aura was blue, concerned with ideas and ideals, might find it replaced by a brilliant green or scarlet as love or passion becomes the overriding purpose of their life.

WHITE

For limitless potential, boundless energy, and life force integration; the colour of the soaring spirit.

White is the colour of divinity and the life force. Associated with both the Sun and Moon, it is also the colour of the Mutable Water sign Pisces. Pythagoras believed that white contained all sound as well as colour. In magic, white represents light, vitality, clear vision and unfettered creativity. In the Oriental world it is the colour of Yang, the pure animus or male energy. As the synthesis of all the other colours, it is the most often seen emanating from the crown of the head.

Unlike the pale colours of an aura that may be drained of energy, true white is vibrant and clear, like liquid crystal, and forms a radiance.

Positive qualities   At its most vibrant this aura is the colour of the innovator and creator, and though not often seen it draws pure light from the cosmos and in return sends forth inner lights of all other colours so that the whole aura will sparkle. It is a highly evolved colour, indicating higher levels of consciousness, purity, and the quest for what is of worth.

Negative aspects   A pale white can suggest a person who is out of touch with the real world, while a murky white reveals feelings of alienation from others.

Physical associations   The vibrant clear aura is one of the integrated mind/body/spirit, of a sense of completeness, good health and an ability to bring healing to groups of people who may be in conflict. White rules the whole body, mind and soul and the interconnectedness between them. White light is a natural pain reliever.

Chakra   Crown.

Crystals/precious stones   Diamond, moonstone, clear crystal quartz, zircon.

Antidote colour   White does not need an antidote colour as it represents the pure life force. If energies get too intense, slow them down with dark purples.

RED

For action, survival, change and for passion; the colour of the crusader.

Red is a magical colour in many traditions, representing blood or the essence of life. Associated in the classical tradition with the planet Mars, the God of War and the Cardinal Fire sign Aries, red is the colour of power, physical energy, courage and determination. Burgundy is the colour of the Fixed Water sign Scorpio, whose meaning is intensity – and more negatively, vengefulness.

Positive qualities   As clear bright red, scarlet or rich ruby, in the aura, it augurs vibrant life, a desire to initiate positive change and a passionate lover.

Negative aspects   When the red is dull or harsh in the aura, it may indicate suppressed fury, resentment and a domineering, vengeful aspect. Dark red without warmth may symbolise irritability and impulsiveness.

Physical associations   As the colour of the life force, a bright red aura can indicate health and strength, the unobstructed flow of the blood, healthy cellular growth and sexual potency. It can especially refer to the feet, hands, skeleton, uterus, penis and vagina. A murky red aura can indicate general infections, blood problems (anaemia may be a dull red) while a harsh red aura indicates a high temperature or soaring blood pressure. Potency problems may be shown as a very pale, flecked red.

Chakra   Root or base.

Crystals/precious stones   Banded red jasper, tiger's eye, obsidian or apache's tears, or any pebble you find with dark reddish brown to black colouring.

Antidote colour (for excess auric red)   Blue

ORANGE

For confidence, joy, independence and strong identity; the colour of the integrator.

Orange is a colour of the Sun and the abundant fruits of the Earth. It is also the colour of both the Fixed Fire sign Leo and the Mutable Fire sign Sagittarius. Orange is the colour of fertility, whether personal or to bring a project to fruition, self-esteem, health, happiness and personal desires.

Positive qualities   A warm rich orange indicates the ability to integrate different aspects of life and assimilate what is of worth. Also, creativity and artistic ability, and an open-minded, enthusiastic and optimistic nature.

Negative aspects   A pale orange can indicate a lack or loss of identity or low self-esteem, while a harsh orange can represent superficiality and eccentric tendencies. Murky orange with cracks can indicate an oversensitive ego.

Physical associations   As the colour of fertility and stimulation, a clear orange aura indicates a regular pulse rate, healthy metabolism and efficient immune system. A cloudy orange can augur allergies, infections in the reproductive system, menstrual pain and sometimes gall bladder problems. Orange especially refers to ovaries, large and small intestines, spleen, adrenal glands, kidneys and muscles.

Chakra   Sacral.

Crystals/precious stones   Amber, beryl, carnelian, coral, jasper or banded orange agate or topaz.

Antidote colour   Indigo.

YELLOW

For logic, the mind and thoughts and knowledge of all kinds; the colour of the communicator.

Yellow is associated with Mercury, the planet named after the Roman winged messenger of the gods, who spanned the dimensions and was also the deity of healing, moneylenders and thieves. So yellow is linked with business acumen and occasionally trickery. It is also the colour of the Mutable Air sign Gemini and the Mutable Fire sign Sagittarius.

Positive qualities   Yellow is the quicksilver colour, when the mind is focused on new ideas or on planning strategies or assimilating knowledge. It is essentially a colour of joy and of clear communication. If the yellow is brilliant, it is a sign of an actor or entertainer, while a clear yellowy-brown augurs a scientific mind.

Negative aspects Irregular, harsh streaks of yellow can indicate hyperactivity, while a mustard yellow may mask jealousy or resentment. A metallic yellow haze conceals secrets, or less than honest intent.

Physical associations A clear bright yellow speaks of a good memory, excellent powers of concentration, a well-functioning lymphatic and nervous system and healthy digestion. A dull yellow can indicate digestive and skin disorders, especially those that are stress-related, nervous exhaustion or tension. Yellow rules the solar plexus, liver and kidneys, the nervous system and joints where rheumatism or arthritis may reside.

Chakra Solar plexus.

Crystals/precious stones Calcite, citrine, golden amber, jasper and soft yellow.

Antidote colour Violet.

GREEN

For love, harmony and concern for the environment; the colour of the child of nature.

Green is the colour of Venus, the Roman Goddess of Love, and so is the colour of the heart, love and emotions. As well as the planet Venus, green is linked to the Mutable Earth sign Virgo and through its fairy connotations, with the ability to attract luck. Those with green in the auras are at one with the natural world.

Positive qualities A rich clear green reveals a loving heart, one who is generous with time, love and money. The possessor of this aura can be trusted because their words come from the heart. Olive green promises new hope, transformation and good humour.

Negative aspects A pale green can suggest emotional dependency. A dull, muddy green can reveal conflicting emotions or an emotional leech. Yellowy green can be a sign of possessiveness and unwarranted jealousy. Lime green can imply stress in current relationships.

Physical associations A clear green is a sign of a low and stable blood pressure, a healthy heart and respiratory system. A metallic green that flickers expresses a tendency to panic attacks and food-related illnesses, while a murky green can reveal a tendency to coughs and colds, chest infections, viruses and bronchial problems. Green rules the heart, lungs, respiratory system, tissue and cell growth and general body regeneration. Emerald green is the colour applied in healing.

Chakra Heart.

Crystals/precious stones Amazonite, aventurine, emerald, jade, malachite, moss agate, olivine and tourmaline.

Antidote colour Neutral and so needs no antidote.

TURQUOISE

For integration of heart and mind, feelings and thought and the synthesis of wisdom and experience; the colour of the Wise Healer.

Turquoise is a very special colour, indicating a highly energised personality, capable of influencing other people in a positive way. People with turquoise in their aura can do many things simultaneously and are good organisers. As the colour of the Age of Aquarius, it also represents the ability to span dimensions.

Positive qualities Indicates an artist, a poet or an innovator, perhaps all three. Those with turquoise in the aura are naturally altruistic and protect the weak.

Negative aspects None.

Physical associations Stimulates and strengthens the

immune system, soothes inflammation, calms nerves and aids healing, soothes asthmatic and general respiratory difficulties and heals skin complaints such as eczema. Turquoise rules the throat, upper back, asthma, respiratory problems and swellings of all kinds. It influences the thyroid gland and is used to restore harmony to the whole body.

Crystals/precious stones Aquamarine, malachite, opal, turquoise.

Chakra Throat and heart.

Antidote colour None needed, as it is such a balanced colour. However, if it makes you too 'spaced out' a warm pink will provide the balance.

BLUE

For ideals, expansion of both perspective and physical horizons and authority; the colour of the seeker after truth.

Like white, blue is the colour of limitless possibilities. The Hindu God Vishnu is depicted with blue skin. In magic it is the colour of sky, male or animus energies, power tempered by idealism and was worn by Odin and other Northern Father/Sky Gods. It is a colour of Jupiter, the planet named after the Roman supreme Father God. Blue is also the colour of planet Earth when seen from space and is the colour of the Cardinal Air sign Libra, and as dark blue the Fixed Air sign Aquarius.

Positive qualities A rich blue indicates an integrated personality, someone who has found the right path in life; also a keen sense of justice, natural powers of leadership and the ability to weigh up the facts before acting or speaking. Bright blue is the colour of the altruist who will put principles before personal gain. Pale blue is the colour of the idealist with a global vision for making the world a better place. Clear blue represents detachment, a good antidote to misplaced passion or irrational anger. A blue verging on indigo shows an ability to communicate telepathically. Blue is like purple and green – a healing colour – associated especially with healing powers transmitted through higher powers whether these are the Higher Self, Guardian Angels or Guides.

Negative aspects A dull blue can represent overconservatism and a concern for the letter rather than the spirit of the law, while a harsh blue can be a sign of someone who is autocratic.

Physical associations A clear or bright blue is a sign of stable blood pressure, of balanced hormones and a regular pulse rate. It soothes pain and cools fevers and inflammation. A dull blue can suggest throat, thyroid or teeth problems or depression; an overactive thyroid is often shown by a murky blue. Harsh metallic blue can reveal a tendency towards migraines, headaches, and in children can be an early warning of incipient teething problems. Blue rules the left side of the brain and the nervous system.

Chakra Throat.

Crystals/precious stones Aquamarine, blue lace agate, lapis lazuli, sapphire, turquoise.

Antidote colour Red.

PURPLE

For inner vision, psychic awareness and spirituality; the colour of the evolving soul.

The various auric shades of purple range from indigo through lilac to violet and are variations of the higher levels of spiritual awareness. On the rainbow spectrum the undifferentiated white light divides into two shades of purple: violet followed by indigo (then blue and green). I have given particular associations to violet and indigo where they differ from the main purple correspondences.

Purple is the royal colour, worn by deities, emperors and kings, and also priests. It is especially sacred to Osiris and Jupiter. In magic it provides a link with higher dimensions, with nobility of the spirit and with inspiration drawn from higher planes of consciousness. People with purple in their auras are often potential spiritual teachers, leaders, and healers – a young child who possesses a purple aura is indeed an *old soul*. Associated with the planet Jupiter, as indigo purple is the astrological colour of the Fixed Air sign Aquarius, as violet the Cardinal Air sign Libra, and as mauve/lavender or pale purple of the Mutable Water sign Pisces. Violet is for clairvoyance, mediumship, spirituality and contact with the evolved self, angelic guides; the colour of the mystic.

This is the highest auric level and merges into white as it is joined to pure cosmic energies.

Indigo: for spiritual healing, for psychic awareness and knowledge of past lives/worlds; the colour of the seer. Many white witches and spell-casters have this colour in their aura.

Positive qualities   Any rich shade of purple indicates a connection with unconscious wisdom and the collective knowledge of humankind. A clear colour talks of intuitive awareness and natural clairvoyant powers, while the paler shades are the auric hues of the weaver of fantasy and inhabitant of magical lands.

Negative aspects   When the auric purple is blurred it implies that its owner is spending too long on daydreams and illusions. A dark colour may indicate that the possessor feels alone.

Physical associations   A rich clear purple says that the mind/body and spirit are working in harmony and that the physical senses merge quite naturally with the psychic ones. A dull or cloudy purple can suggest a tendency towards eye and ear infections, headaches, insomnia and nightmares. Purple rules the right side of the brain, the eyes and ears and the sinuses, the scalp and all aspects of pregnancy and childbirth.

Chakra   Brow or Third Eye. (Violet's chakra is the Crown.)
Crystals/precious stones   Amethyst, bornite, peacock's eye, fluorite, purple kunzite, sodalite, sugilite.
Antidote colour   For indigo it is orange. Violet's antidote colour is yellow.

PINK

For unconditional love, reconciliation and gentleness; the colour of the wise counsellor.

Pink is another of Venus's colours and the colour of the Fixed Earth sign Taurus. It represents the gentler aspects of love and kindness. In magic, it is the colour of reconciliation, harmony and of spiritual love expressed through relationships. The aura of a spiritual leader such as Sai Baba, who manifests his love through clean water and hospital projects, appears pink.

Positive qualities   The possessor of a clear pink aura will be a natural peacemaker and friend to all who are vulnerable. He/she will have special affinities with children and animals and will nurture others from when he or she is a child. It is a good aura to detect in others if you are seeking a reconciliation or have personal problems and are feeling vulnerable.
Negative aspects   A harsh pink can augur sentimentality and occasionally over-possessiveness in relation to family and especially children. An almost transparent pink may show emotional exhaustion, perhaps due to giving too much emotionally while counselling others. If the pink is misty, you may be dealing with someone who sees other people's point of view so much that he or she is unlikely to reach any decisions without firm direction. Coral pink is a sign of unrequited love.
Physical associations   A vibrant pink aura signifies balanced emotions, regular sleep patterns, and the ability to

remain relaxed, even in challenging situations, as well as innate healing abilities, especially in children and animals. A harsh pink can reveal a tendency to headaches and earache, while a very transparent pink is a sign of physical as well as emotional exhaustion. Pink rules the head, the glands and all illnesses with psychosomatic origin. It is associated with all family ills and those connected with babies and children.

Crystals/precious stones Coral, kunzite, rhodochrosite, rose quartz, sugilite, tourmaline.

Chakra Heart.

Antidote colour Pink needs no antidote colour, as it exudes gentle loving energies, but if you find you are becoming too sentimental, pastel blue will restore the balance without being too harsh.

BROWN

For nurturing powers, acceptance of frailty in self and others, and earthing power; the colour of the builder of firm foundations.

Brown is the colour of the Earth and the Earth spirits. In magic, it is the colour of affinity with the natural world and acts as a protective force. It is also the colour of the Mother Goddesses and of Saturn, Old Father Time, God and the planet of Fate, the reality principle and the passage of time. Astrologically it is the colour of the Cardinal Earth sign Capricorn.

Positive qualities Brown is a very complex colour, with different auric meanings according to its shade and intensity. Rich golden brown can indicate a person deeply rooted in Mother Earth, a keen environmentalist or lover of the land and countryside, or a person who is establishing new roots in a practical way. A warm brown is the colour of the nurturer.

A deep brown is the colour of practical and instinctive wisdom.

Negative aspects   Murky brown can indicate narrow horizons and sometimes over-indulgence, while a harsh brown can be present in the aura of someone who is obsessed with money or material concerns.

Physical associations   A rich brown is indicative of a store of physical energy and primal strength. A dull shade can indicate an overload of work and stress and maybe blocked chakras. Brown rules the feet, the legs, the hands, the skeleton and the large intestine.

Chakra   Root or base.

Crystals/precious stones   Amber, desert rose, leopardskin or snakeskin jasper, rutilated quartz, tiger's eye.

Antidote colour   Brown needs no antidote colour because it is so earthed, but if you feel weighed down a little orange will lighten the mood.

BLACK

For transitions, regeneration, acceptance of life as it is and the confrontation of mortality; the colour of the transformer.

Though black is a colour associated with death and mourning in the modern Westernised world, it is primarily a colour of total acceptance. The Yin or female principle in Oriental spirituality is as vital for existence as its polarity Yang, the light principle. Like brown, black is ruled by the planet Saturn and the astrological Cardinal Earth sign Capricorn. Black is also linked with regeneration. In Ancient Egypt the black silt of the Nile brought new life each year and black cats were especially sacred. In magic, black is the colour of endings that carry within them seeds of new beginnings.

Positive qualities   A clear black, almost transparent aura may indicate that a person is resting emotionally and spiritually, perhaps after an exhausting or stressful period, and so is growing stronger behind the protective darkness. Because psychic protection is so strongly implicated in a positive black aura, the possessor may deliberately or spontaneously be shielding him or herself from intrusion, so this is not a subject to be read.

Negative aspects   A matt black indicates exhaustion or depression, but is more usually seen as black spots or streaks than as a blanket aura. However, a harsh metallic black can suggest that the person is potentially a psychic vampire, who will offload problems but ignore any positive suggestions and make the most negative interpretation of the motives and actions of others – an aura to avoid.

Physical associations   The presence of black spots in the aura may indicate that some part of the body is imbalanced or energies are not flowing freely. This may mean that the person has some negative habits that he or she should work on. Meditation helps reduce these spots, as do things like exercise and sunlight. Black rules the feet, the legs, the bones and the large intestine.

Chakra   Root or base.

Crystals/precious stones   Smoky quartz, jet, obsidian and onyx.

Antidote colour   Pure, white light.

GREY

For compromise, adaptability and the ability to merge into the background; the colour of the keeper of many secrets.

Grey is ruled by Saturn and some say it is the hidden aspect of Mercury when he becomes invisible. Pale grey is the colour of the Mutable Air sign Gemini. It is the colour of keeping one's counsel and maintaining a low profile at times when to do otherwise would be unwise.

Positive qualities   Like black, grey can be created when the possessor wishes to remain unobserved, and on page 102 I describe how to create an aura of grey as a form of protection. A silvery dove grey is an aura seen in peacemakers. It indicates at least neutrality in a hostile situation, but according to the clarity of the hue, perhaps an ally. There is willingness to compromise and to find a way around difficulties when grey appears in an aura.

Negative aspects   A dull grey may suggest depression, while a very pale grey can be a symbol of indecision and an unwillingness to challenge the status quo, even if it is unjust.

Physical associations   A clear dove grey is a good sign of a person not easily given to stress and so possessing a stable constitution. A very pale or dull grey can demonstrate a depleted energy store and so the immune system may not be as effective as usual. Grey rules the subconscious mind and the bones and the etheric body.

Chakra   Root.

Crystals/precious stones   Smoky quartz, apache's tears, banded agate.

Antidote colour   Grey needs no antidote as it is completely neutral, but if you start to feel confused a little silver light will penetrate the mist.

SILVER

For mystery and feminine intuitive wisdom, also of gentle gradual growth or increase.

Silver is the colour of the Moon and lunar Goddesses Isis and Diana. Astrologically, silver is the colour of Cancer, the Cardinal Water sign. It represents dreams, visions and a desire for fulfilment beyond the material world. Silver in magic represents intuition and sudden insights, especially in dreams. It is the aura of one who, given encouragement, may become a star.

Positive qualities   Silver stars or sparks in an aura indicate hidden potential, mystery and secrets of a kind that are exciting and will, when revealed, bring joy. Silver in an aura can indicate pregnancy or a time when conception is possible, but it can equally refer to the seeds of imagination, creativity and awakening or re-awakening sexuality.

Negative aspects   Metallic flashes can be a sign of someone who is seeking to create an illusion or image or craves excitement and stimulation.

Physical associations   Silver indicates the healthy regulation of bodily fluids and the ability to eliminate impurities and pain from the body. A matt distended silver aura can be a sign of fluid retention and the inability to move on psychologically from the past. Silver rules the cycles of the body, especially female ones.

Chakra   Brow.

Crystals/precious stones   Haematite, moonstones, rose quartz.

Antidote colour   Gold, the colour of solar light.

GOLD

For perfection, immortality and peak experiences; the colour of the visionary.

Gold is the colour of the Sun and the solar gods and goddesses, for example the Egyptian Ra or Re who each morning began his journey across the heavens in his solar boat, and at night, in the form of a ram-headed man, passed through the underworld to emerge in the east in the morning. It is associated with the astrological Fixed Fire sign Leo. Gold is not often seen in auras and you can be sure that if a child has a golden aura he or she is destined to be a very special person and will achieve fame and fortune.

Positive qualities   Gold is the colour of the seer and of the visionary, and one whose life will change the world in a positive way.

Negative aspects   A harsh gold can indicate an obsession with power and a desire for worldly wealth at any cost.

Physical associations   Gold indicates long life, and as the most powerful healing colour health and vitality and the natural regenerative qualities of body and mind. A tarnished gold may suggest a tendency towards addictions, obsessions and compulsions. Gold rules the nervous system, spine and skin.

Chakra   The whole chakra system.

Crystals/precious stones   Amber, citrine, tiger's eye and topaz.

Antidote colour   The silver light of lunar power.

USING A CRYSTAL PENDULUM TO IDENTIFY THE COLOURS IN THE AURA

In Chapter 8 I describe how you can use a crystal pendulum on a chain to identify dark spots or holes and fill them with pure crystalline light.

Pendulum dowsing has been used with great success by oil companies to discover the best place to drill wells. But it is equally effective when applied to the personal sphere. Pendulums are controlled by unconscious movements of the arm that are guided by psychokinetic energy to reveal information accessible only on a psychic level. The pendulum is one of the most accurate methods of reading auras, especially your own, using a technique called *map* or *remote dowsing*.

Map or remote dowsing means identifying factors about a place or person by creating a map or diagram to represent the actual sphere or focus and holding a pendulum over the representation (see my book *Pendulum Dowsing* (Piatkus) for a detailed description of this technique). Map dowsing is also a good method of giving absent healing.

If you are not familiar with a pendulum, start by discovering its personal yes/positive and no/negative response. You can either gently set your pendulum in motion or allow it to start moving of its own volition. Frequently, a clockwise circle or ellipse forms the 'Yes' response, and this response remains consistent once established, whether the pendulum is used for questions about health, happiness or money, or for tracking water, lost objects or even ghosts.

Since our emotions are a trigger and a channel for successful pendulum divination, to find your personal 'Yes' response visualise a very happy moment, a success or a peak experience when you suddenly mastered a skill or reached the top of a high mountain, either actually or symbolically, and felt a surge of joy. The pendulum will respond to the recalled positive emotion with a 'Yes' response.

A negative pendulum movement is generally the mirror image of the 'Yes' response, for example an anti-clockwise circle or ellipse. But your personal pendulum's 'No' may be entirely different. Discover this by concentrating on a moment when you were disappointed or failed to reach the peak of your particular mountain, and as you momentarily recall your sadness your pendulum will move on its anti-clockwise path. Follow this rapidly with another happy recollection and your pendulum will express positivity once more.

Exercise: Using a pendulum to identify colours in the aura

- *Wait until you are calm, relaxed and a little sleepy and have a bath to which a few drops of sandalwood or ylang-ylang essential oil are added to gently awaken your psychic powers.*

- *Light incense or scented candles in the room you are using for the exercise.*

- *Draw a circle and divide it into all the auric colours, beginning with white and following through the colours so that you end with gold. Include different shades of colours – many children's crayon and watercolour sets have an amazing array. Use only clear colours; the pendulum will identify any disorders by a negative movement. If you make the chart on stiff card and laminate it, you can use it for future aura analysis and healing. Note your findings so you can analyse them afterwards.*

- *First concentrate on establishing your predominant auric colour. Beginning at the top of the circle, ask the pendulum to identify by a positive response the predominant permanent personal auric colour. Addressing your pendulum, even silently, may feel strange, but you are defining the parameters of the search.*

- *Move the pendulum around the circle slowly and pause over each segment. You do not need to set the pendulum in motion, as each segment is a separate task. Your pendulum may give a negative response in the other segments or remain motionless. If more than one segment is identified, see in which one the pendulum moves most vigorously. The second one may be a subsidiary strand.*

- *Beginning again at the top of the circle, ask your pendulum to identify the current predominant mood colour in your aura – this may not be the one you expected. Again, the pendulum may identify a subsidiary colour.*

- *Next ask your pendulum to identify any auric colours in which there are dark spots, tears, holes or potential negativity, this time by a negative response. At this point, you may see either externally, or in your mind's eye, the particular shade become murky, metallic or fade. The pendulum may return to one of your predominant colours if there are any blockages. If it does not react adversely everything is fine. If there are negative responses, note them.*

- *When you have finished, write or sketch your findings, then without conscious thought write an analysis as though for someone else, allowing the colours to suggest images and words.*

- *Afterwards, look through the basic colour meanings in this chapter, and see how you have expanded upon them. Aura reading is not about meanings that are true for all people, but as with Tarot reading or any other intuitive art, are only the focus for your own natural clairvoyance.*

- *Keep a record of your findings and see how your aura changes over time and under different circumstances.*

- *When you have finished, circle your pendulum in an anti-clockwise movement over your head to remove negative energies, then nine times clockwise to energise your body and mind. If any colours were very dull or pale, use crystals or candles of similar colours and breathe in the coloured light to restore positive energies.*

Chapter 4

HOW TO INTERPRET AURAS

We can read the auras of others and gain useful insights without probing too deeply into an individual's private world. Just as you would not attempt to mind-read the secret thoughts of strangers or colleagues through telepathy, but would intuit a mood or perhaps an unspoken request for help, so you can use auras to detect the moods and needs of others and create positive interactions (see also Chapter 5). If someone's aura is misty and clouded with grey, or very dark, accept that it is off limits. In-depth aura reading is a very intimate divinatory art that involves a great deal of trust between reader and subject.

For everyday purposes you need only to study the two predominant aspects of the aura that I have already mentioned: the relatively permanent auric colour that is visible when a subject is relaxed and there are no stimuli – the personal or root aura – and the aura of the current mood. You may see one or both according to circumstances.

These can, in practice, be easily distinguished by the intensity and stability of colour. The mood aura is much more transient and the colour more ethereal and full of movement, flickers, flashes and twinkles, while the root aura colour is more matt and solid. When you meet a stranger, what you will see is the auric colour of the current mood, though you may see a more permanent colour in the background if the person is fairly relaxed – occasionally a person's basic auric set is so strong that only in extreme circumstances will it change.

If you think of different levels and auric colours as mingling, you may see streaks of different colours either shining through or superimposed on the predominant auric colour, if the person is going through a period of change. People sometimes say, '*I knew at once he/she was in a sunny mood*' or '*he/she had the black dog of depression hanging over him/her*', and this knowledge is transmitted through colours, even before the person is close enough for us to see their facial expression or observe their body language.

Looking through a window at work and seeing the aura of an important client, or employer, or a visitor to your home, is an excellent forewarning of either potential hazards or opportunities and gives you time to adjust and/or protect your own aura.

Using the colour meanings given in the previous chapter, you can begin to interpret the auras of those around you and will find the more you do work with auras, the more natural the ability becomes. The methods given in Chapter 2 are very effective when you are working with another person in depth, or for reading your own aura or the auras of others in controlled circumstances with the right lighting and when you have plenty of time to make your observations.

But in practice, much aura interpretation needs to be instantaneous, with less than ideal lighting and perhaps distracting noise. The advantage of instant aura reading is that you do not have time to rationalise or doubt the evidence of your clairvoyant eye. In this chapter I suggest a number of fast techniques for a variety of situations that work well even for those new to aura reading. All of them work through the medium of a physical phenomenon as a way of kick-starting psychic vision, and each takes no more than a minute, so that you do not give the impression of staring. After two or three weeks, your ability to see and sense auras will become so evolved that you can discard largely artificial methods.

THE PSYCHIC CAMERA/FLASHBULB TECHNIQUE

This is my favourite method and is valuable when you are studying a particular subject over a period of days or weeks and want to accurately monitor changes, but are not able to work within a relaxed time frame.

In psychology, it has for a number of years been recognised that while the human memory normally *tidies up* recollections, even in a short space of time, the *flashbulb* memory preserves even minute details, for example what a person was doing the moment they heard of the Moon landing, J. F. Kennedy's assassination or Princess Diana's death. Even years later people can recall in detail that moment which is frozen in time by the intensity of the emotion generated.

The same technique can be applied to auras; you freeze the perception of the aura by building up an intensity of feeling around the image. Your subject can be across the other side of a room or even outdoors, perhaps watching a sporting event or waiting at a bus stop or on a railway or Tube station. The only proviso is that he or she is motionless.

- *Frame your subject either against natural sunlight, with an artificial light or in candlelight. You need only capture one part of the aura in your psychic viewfinder, so look either to the side or slightly above or beyond the subject to avoid the impression of staring.*

- *Visualise the light increasing in intensity so that the whole outline of the head/body becomes pure white and, as you do so, connect with the power of the light and feel it rising within you.*

- *Breathe in the light, hold it for a count of one and two and three, and as you exhale, project the light towards the aura so that it becomes brighter and more intense – feel the bubble of light growing within you as you continue to inhale and exhale.*

- *Continue to breathe in this way for about a minute, increasing the intensity with each breath. Then, when you can feel the white light pulsating, project a final flash of light from your mind to the image, freezing the aura image within the intense power and whiteness. Momentarily, you may see white light circling the aura like a camera flashbulb, as your power meets the outer auric field – you have not affected the aura at all, merely touched it with the light.*

- *The image will remain frozen in your mind until you are able to draw it on a piece of paper, colouring or painting the outline you have created.*

- *Work fast without thinking – you may see both current mood and, if the person is not focused, the permanent colour of the root aura. More than one mood colour may indicate that two different aspects are at present either complementary or in conflict; harmonious shades would suggest the former.*

USING A CD OR A CD ROM DISC/THIN METALLIC SURFACE

This works either for capturing your own aura or that of another person in close proximity. Remember that you can aura read using the back of the head, and this is ideal either at a social occasion where music is playing, or in a workplace where there is computer equipment – anywhere in which holding a CD Rom would not seem strange. The image of the face or head will be distorted, but in the hologram effect of the silver metal you will see the flash of auric colour using the colours of the physical rainbow that are evoked. Of course you are using a physical phenomenon, but the rainbow light will react with and amplify the person's natural auric colours. That you are not merely picking up a physical phenomenon is demonstrated by the fact that under the same light, and in the same position, you will see different auras for different people in rapid succession. Think of the method as a rapid trigger for your own slower powers. It is particularly effective for capturing relatively transient or emotionally altered auras.

- *This method works best in either strong artificial light or sunshine. Experiment with catching rainbow light in the silvery* surface. Now tip the CD or CD Rom so that you capture an image in it – either your own or that of another person. If the centre of the CD or CD Rom is approximately focused at the middle of the face or back of the head, the aura will appear above and around the head.

- Thin silver foil also works well, if it is anchored to a firm surface. One of the best surfaces I used was a silver foil gift bag.

- This is easy to do while you are sitting talking as someone approaches.

- Again at a suitable point record the aura, using paints or colouring pencils.

THE PSYCHIC HANDSHAKE

People reveal a great deal about themselves by the way they shake hands. It is also an effective method of aura reading since the hands and the palms are areas, like the head, around which the aura can be perceived clearly. In Chapter 2, you carried out an exercise in which you held your hands against a dark background with the fingers and palms almost touching each other, then moved them apart quickly. The auric energy you saw between the fingers can also be created by a handshake.

Just before shaking hands with someone, gently move your hands together, palms facing but not quite touching each other, until you feel the auric energy and maybe lights, sparks or colours building up. This way your own auric power is sensitised and will be receptive to the auric impressions of the other person, but is sufficiently strong so as not to be drawn towards the other person immediately. Thus you get a pure impression.

Grasp the other person's hand very lightly so that he or she is applying the pressure, and look at the colours emanating from their fingers. You have only a second or two before your own auric energies respond and mingle – the joining of energies through hands is a good way of monitoring the two-way effect of more formal relationships.

The most important impressions are those you feel through your fingertips – true psychometry. These impressions will translate into colours either internally in your mind or externally around the subject's hands, and you may also pick up the emotions, needs and even health of the other person in words or images as well as colours. There may be a tingling sensation, harsh if the person is feeling hostile or threatened, warm for a positive encounter, or weak if the subject lives mainly in his or her own world or has many people constantly drawing energy off him/her.

Though an instant exercise, it forms a good transition for more in-depth work.

USING INSTANT COLOUR DOWSING

This is the easiest and most abstract form of instant aura interpretation. This time, however, you will not dowse with a crystal pendulum but with the index finger of your power hand (the one you write with). You are once again adopting the remote dowsing method whereby auric impressions are transferred to colour representations.

Because you need to work rapidly you are not seeking the yes/no response, but the more direct gravitational pull that is frequently used when dowsing to decide between a number of options. The sensation has been described as a heaviness or a pressure downwards towards a particular option. I have seen this demonstrated by countless people who have made up their minds on a conscious level, but whose hand has guided them to a previously unconsidered choice that subsequently proves to be the route to happiness or success.

In aura reading, you can use the gravitational pull to identify predominant auric colours using the colour lists from the previous chapter, but in practice three-dimensional objects seem to give a more rapid response for instant dowsing. The method works through tactile contact.

There are may different materials you can use to provide a

range of colours; choose the one that fits in with the context of the aura reading. Any colour selection can form the focus, from children's building blocks to a colour swatch from a fashion store. For example, you could have an array of different coloured crystals, pencils, wool, embroidery silks or sewing threads, buttons, beads, flowers in a vase or garden, anything that will not look incongruous in the setting. The person whose aura you are reading can thus either be at a distance or close by, and as long as you are still, forming a focal point, he or she can move around or be motionless. With a moving auric image, you may see colours around the hands and feet as well as the head, and these seem to swirl around almost in the shape, not of the static person but of the moving body.

Crystals are especially effective as they contain living energies to attract the body's innate dowsing powers, and some people do keep a dish of different coloured crystals either at home or in the workplace for this form of auric interpretation.

Exercise: Colour dowsing

- *Focus for a few seconds on the area around the person's head if he or she is still, or around the extremities of the body if they are moving.*

- *Now cast your eyes beyond and above the head, but do not consciously try to register colours.*

- *As you do so, without looking circle your index finger in a clockwise circle, just touching the different colours. Even if you feel vibrations in your fingers, do not make a selection.*

- *Look away or down and then up again at the area around the subject's head.*

- *As you do so this time, again without looking, allow your index finger to guide your hand towards one colour and select this. You will feel your finger pulling down as though it is heavier than the rest of the hand, or you may experience a tingling sensation when the finger touches the appropriate colour.*

- *Do not try to rationalise, but note the shade.*
- *This represents the colour of the current auric mood.*
- *Return the selected colour to the others; occasionally the current and root auric colours are the same.*
- *Look once more towards the aura and, as you do so, allow your index finger to circle and touch the colours once more and let impressions form in your mind. You may find that as you look around the area of the head, colours and patterns are spontaneously forming – they usually do when you are not trying. This information will help you to interpret more clearly the divinatory colours you select.*
- *Allow your index finger to pull down or vibrate over a second colour, which may be the same as the first, but is not usually. This gives the more permanent or root auric colour that indicates the guiding quality when the person is relaxed.*
- *Look up and let your index finger move over the colours a third time to see whether another colour is present. Occasionally, if a person's life is in flux, there may be a variety of streaks.*
- *If you select black or grey as a tertiary colour, this may indicate holes or dark spots.*
- *When you have the opportunity, using colouring pencils or paints in the divinatory colours you have selected, allow your hand to create the auric picture. Your hand will automatically insert any dark places in the correct location.*

MONITORING THE AURAS OF OTHERS

While reading auras in absolutely any situation is the best way to become proficient, it is also important to develop your in-depth interpretation skills. In addition to reading about the meanings of different auric colours and levels in this and other books, the best way to become adept is by monitoring particular auras over a period of time so that you can discover for yourself how different circumstances can create different auric responses. Before long, this will cease to be a conscious exercise and you will discover that you are automatically detecting regular patterns in the auras of those with whom you regularly interact.

Select someone close in your personal world and a second person with whom you have more formal but frequent contact, and for the first reading try to observe them when they are relaxed. Do this for two or three days and you should identify their root or personal auric colour (the one that is always present).

Observe your subjects at least twice a week, every day if possible, at different times and in different situations. You may see a variety of mood auras. An initial glance will give you that first accurate moment of intuition – scribble down the colours and brief notes of the date, time and any unusual circumstances. You may find certain times and events cause particular auric change, for example a visit to a difficult rela-tion or an evening devoted to a favourite activity. If there are any particular lows, try to find out by tactful questioning what is happening, even in seemingly unrelated spheres of that person's life.

It is only if these colours never vary that you need to be aware that there may be a certain fixed nature that can make interactions difficult. Equally, if an aura changes at every encounter, then you may be dealing with someone who tries to please whoever he or she is with.

INTERPRETING AURAS – APPLYING THE SKILL TO THE EVERYDAY WORLD

Once you can see different colours and know their meanings, you can begin to use aura interpretation as a way of using your psychic knowledge in the everyday world. As well as seeing or sensing colours, the process involves all your psychic senses and is simply a question of listening to your inner voice and trusting your clairvoyant eye.

To return to the window scenario: your immediate boss draws up in the car. It is quite an important day as you need to ask for special leave, promotion or have a project you are anxious to initiate – is this a good day to ask?

Nadia's Aura Reading

Nadia, who is in her thirties, works for Alison, a female executive in her early fifties, in advertising. She had the opportunity to go to the Far East for a month, all expenses paid, with her partner, who had suddenly been asked to take on a work project there.

Would Alison be amenable to Nadia taking all her holiday in one go almost immediately, as there would have to be a major rearrangement of schedules? Nadia had been observing Alison's aura over a period of weeks and noticed that, unusually for an executive in a hard-selling business, her aura was predominantly purple, a colour of spirituality and higher powers. This was reflected in the fact that the agency was well known for its integrity and very ethereal advertisements that had proved extremely popular in promoting a variety of services. Alison was also respected by her employees since she always took into account their personal needs and ensured that the atmosphere, although creative, was calm.

But today, unusually, Alison's aura was a flickering metallic red, a sign that indicated she was under great stress and was feeling fearful. Nadia's intuition tuned into images of a secure pillar being shaken and an earth tremor reverberating through a temple. She also saw a beautiful deer, whom she identified as Alison, running in all directions to escape the tremor and heard the words '*Calm her motion and the tremor will cease*'.

Nadia therefore cancelled all calls and took tea into Alison's office, at first talking quietly and generally about successful projects. As Nadia continued talking softly to Alison, Alison explained that during an apparently routine weekly meeting with the firm's most lucrative client Simon, out of the blue he had demanded an entirely new and more dynamic approach to a long-running but successful campaign. He had given Alison two months to plan a completely original and exotic strategy for his electrical goods chain. This was totally out of character for him and for the agency. If she was unable to deliver, he threatened to take his account, more than a third of the firm's profit, to another agency. Simon accused Alison of losing her grasp on the current market and being too unfocused.

Nadia realised that this apparently unwelcome catalyst might actually fit in with her plans as she could research Oriental cultures for the new campaign, in a fast-changing area that was still rooted in the timeless wisdom of the Orient. However, the jagged streaks that had entirely masked Alison's usually purple aura made Nadia realise that now was not the time to press her advantage or to further disrupt routine by proposing taking her annual leave. Alison, in her unusually volatile state, might feel that Nadia was trying to manipulate her or that she was acting irresponsibly in going away when the firm was in crisis. However, the new rising energies as the red began to clear during the long discussion instinctively felt good, like a red dust storm clearing away the debris – survival was the auric theme that Alison took home.

The next day, Alison's aura was bright yellow – she had spent the night on facts, figures and strategies and was eager to brainstorm for new ideas. *Yellow* is the auric antidote for purple, and Nadia – and Alison herself – realised that Alison was losing the drive and sense of fun that had made the all-female firm so successful originally. The yellow aura was sparkling and Nadia could see in the colour images of huge sunflowers rapidly pushing towards the light, a golden river flowing and growing wider. Alison's energies were centred on ideas and her natural creativity shone through, but there was still no purple, so Nadia knew that appealing to her sensitivity and her natural concern for the welfare of her staff would not work; Alison was in business mode.

So Nadia drew up a proposal of ideas based on the Orient, with designs of exotic lanterns, firecrackers and the festivals of light that were a feature of Hong Kong's culture. She added in a memo that her husband was going on a trip to Hong Kong and that Nadia could go, all expenses paid, to research the concept on behalf of the agency, but stressed that this was only one option. She also set up a viable plan for work cover if she was away so that the agency could run as normal.

Alison accepted the suggestions enthusiastically, and though Nadia took the time as holiday, she used her travel to create a new, exciting theme that retained the key account for the agency. When Nadia returned from her trip abroad, she discovered that Alison had repainted the office buttercup yellow – and Nadia's predominant root aura had also changed from purple to yellow.

The situation worked well because Nadia had been studying auras for some time and avoided a potential flash point. But an instant interpretation can work just as well with someone entirely new, if you rely on your intuition, your inner voice and internal imagery system to give you the personal meaning that standard colours assume for an individual in a particular situation.

INTERPRETING YOUR OWN AURA

Studying your own aura is altogether more relaxed, and in the previous two chapters I have suggested ways of seeing your own aura. Although we may think we are in touch with our moods and feelings, it can be very helpful to monitor your own aura at regular intervals, initially when you are relaxed, then after a quarrel, after making love, after a success at work or home, and when you are sad, tired, enervated and sleepy. The instant methods in this chapter can also be adapted so that you study the auric colours around your fingers or select colours as you look at your aura in a mirror.

Keep a special mirror for looking at your own aura. This need be no larger than a hand mirror. Charge it initially by sprinkling a circle of sea salt clockwise around the mirror for the protection of the ancient Element of the Earth.

Pass the smoke of a lighted frankincense or myrrh incense stick (for the Air element) around the mirror nine times in a clockwise direction. Frankincense is empowering and myrrh healing and protective.

Now circle your mirror with a gold candle clockwise and a silver candle anti-clockwise for the Element of Fire and the power of the Sun and Moon.

Finally, create sacred water by stirring a few grains of sea salt into a dish of rainwater collected before the rain touched the ground. This represents the Water element. Make a circle of water around the mirror by sprinkling drops in a clockwise direction. Your mirror is now empowered and protected for aura work.

Place your mirror where sunlight falls around it – not upon it – or where candlelight is reflected not directly in the glass but to create a glow. Sit slightly to the side so that your face is not reflected directly but sufficiently close so that your auric glow is captured in the glass. If you find this difficult, a swing mirror gently tilted can help to catch physical light in the glass that will act as an amplifier for auric energies.

Note down the colours. Try this for two or three weeks to get a representative pattern. Two equal strands in your root aura, for example, blue for thought and green for feelings, would, if the colours are clear, suggest a balanced approach. If they are muddy, it may be that you are having problems integrating the different aspects of your personality to your present world.

Exercise: Making a simple auragram

You can create this either for yourself or for someone with whom you interact daily, in a formal or informal relationship.

It is an effective way to record auras and enables you to make direct comparisons and analyse your findings.

- *Photocopy or scan the diagram below, or create your own either by hand or on a computer.*
- *The key to a successful auragram is spontaneity. Fill in the colour quickly and add stars, streaks, etc. by allowing your hand to place them. If you try to plan the colour formation in detail before drawing it, you interfere with the psychic imprint that your subconscious mind will express if unfettered.*

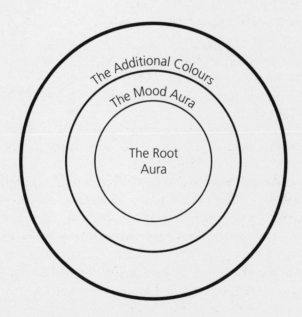

A simple auragram

- *The innermost circle represents the predominant root aura – if you do not pick this up from the aura of a stranger or acquaintance, leave it blank, although you may see it or intuit it, for example by the dowsing method suggested on page 53. With someone you do know, the auric root colour you observe when he or she is relaxed is unlikely to change in the short term, but as with the example of Nadia and Alison, challenging or direction-changing events can cause the permanent aura to alter. During the transition, this circle may contain streaks of the emerging colour. If the colour in this innermost circle changes frequently, the subject may be easily influenced by others.*

- *The second mood aura circle enclosing the inner one is more transient, but also the most influential in aura inter-pretation, especially in encounters with strangers or officials you do not know well. The mood colour tells you how to react. If you get little change here, the person concerned may be very set in their ways.*

- *The outermost circle is for any tertiary colours, whether a second strand of the permanent aura or conflicting or harmonising moods. Use symbols to indicate connections. You can also record here any flashes of colours (there may be several) as either bands or segments. Record any stars, jagged lines of darkness or dark spots in the appropriate circle.*

You can create auragrams anywhere – on the backs of envelopes, as doodles on a notepad, even with your paint programme on the computer. If you keep a record of aura-grams, you can arrange them in rows so that you can begin to detect the patterns. Later they can form a progress chart for the effects of healing or aura strengthening work.

Chapter 5

AURAS AND RELATIONSHIPS

Our energy fields are linked with those we love, with friends and others with whom we are in close contact and also in more formal relationships, for example in the workplace or when dealing with officials. Energies pass between two auras, or more in a group who regularly interact, whether in a family, social, learning or work situation.

Positive auric interactions are reflected in harmonious relationships in the everyday world. Where a relationship is loving, the auras merge at the head and heart levels, whereas possessiveness or manipulation tend to seep through every level of the auric field.

You can observe positive auric connections by looking initially at the head and heart levels of two people who have a close emotional and physical relationship – a mother and child, two lovers, or a couple who have been married for many years. This is easiest to perceive if the people are standing or sitting physically close to each other. If the rays are clear and bright or in gentle pastels all is well, but if there seems to be seepage or murkiness there may be underlying tensions.

Equally, aura readings may reveal two-way tendrils of mutual dependency in a seemingly victim/villain scenario. A man or woman may declare that he or she only stays with a partner for the sake of the children, or constantly complains to a partner about an over-possessive parent. Sometimes the little boy/girl inside is clinging to the parent or playing a power game that causes a partner to compete for affection – auric murkiness, knots and tendrils will reveal the true story.

Study colleagues at work, or perhaps an employer and employee between whom there is great open antipathy. There may be dark spots or tears, or one aura may become significantly paler or less vibrant and the weaker of the two leak colour and energy which is absorbed by the stronger. Also monitor the friend or colleague who suffers one disaster after another and to whom everyone lends a sympathetic ear. You may discover that the aura of the person you thought to be the passive victim is actually drawing strength from the friend or colleague who is acting as counsellor. You may see the energy being drawn across as though by suction by this psychic vampire.

What can also be significant is the strength of rays travelling between people whom you thought did not really interact. Vibes travelling one way may be positive or tinged with envy and resentment, an unconscious form of psychic attack.

THE AURA OF LOVE

About 75 per cent of relationship friction comes from temporary auric mismatch in which one or both partners are unaware of the auric indicators that precede and are not as easily masked as non-verbal signals. The predominant mood and current concerns of a partner or potential lover are reflected in the aura. This can indicate whether positive interaction lies in gentle communication, distraction by moving to neutral territory or topics, or whether this is a good time for a heart to heart or confrontation. A temporarily fractured eggshell ego, reflected as a murky, patchy orange aura, is obviously not going to respond to a tirade about unpaid bills or a demand for support in a family dispute. It is not a question of constantly making concessions, but not embarking upon issues at a time when the other person is totally unresponsive – literally on another wavelength.

Much of this is true with any close relationship between

family members and friends, especially when a relationship is developing and therefore vulnerable, or where there are longstanding areas of dispute, where tensions come from outside the auric relationship under scrutiny. You may even see rays entering the aura like arrows from an unidentified source.

Understanding what is happening is a large part of the battle. However, since every encounter is made up of the joint auric vibrations of you and the other person, you can improve any situation or maximise a particularly responsive phase in the other person by modifying your own aura, either with an antidote colour or some modifying shade so that the joint aura is one which offers the best atmosphere for loving and creative interactions. You are not interfering with the aura of the other person; think of the auric adjustment as preparing a room for a lover, friend or colleague. You might turn down harsh lighting, play soothing music, light a fire if it was a cold day, scatter bright cushions, or tidy up to create a businesslike atmosphere. Only if you are regularly having to modify your aura should you question the suitability of the situation.

Sometimes, if there is no way of avoiding a challenge or a person is consistently being autocratic or indecisive, you may need to strengthen your own aura to steer the direction of an interaction towards a necessary discussion – and result. Later in this chapter, I suggest ways of modifying and also of strengthening your own auric colours so that you are not depressed by a partner's black mood and don't give way to the emotional pressure or unjustifiable anger of others. Firstly, I have listed possible interpretations of different colours in terms of a relationship and suggested antidote and strengthening colours. In practice, the two functions are virtually interchangeable.

These are only guides and as you become more experienced, you will not even be aware of your aura adapting to different scenarios. In social and work situations, you may find that you are dealing with a collective aura, but the principle of altering the balance is the same.

COLOURS AND RELATIONSHIPS

White

Love　This colour creates a powerful aura that at its clearest and brightest enables a relationship to reach great heights of physical, mental and spiritual unity, in which there are no boundaries and no barriers to total union. However, if you are seeking a more intimate encounter, you may need to slow down or modify the auric flow with a gentle pink or green, as well as yellow to give direction to the outpouring of energy.

Family and friends　This is a very healing and inspirational colour and so any interaction will be dynamic, stimulating and constantly suggest new possibilities for mutual exploration. A murky white may reflect a sense of alienation from others that will need golden brown input to restore connection.

Business　Each day is a new adventure and relationships will never stagnate – only a very pale misty white indicates unrealistic expectations and dreams that need to be countered with a blast of bright yellow logic and again golden brown for grounding.

Red

Love　This is the aura of sexuality and pure passion, if the red is clear and bright. If you feel the need for a gentler form of love, clear pastel green or pink will introduce an element of deeper connection, while purple will add a spiritual dimension, perfect for tantric sex. If a partner's scarlet aura is tinged with neon flares and the lust is not directed your way, you may need to monitor your hunter/huntress's unexplained absences more carefully. A muddied red can indicate thoughts of straying passion, an early warning system for partners.

Family and friends   A dark red can indicate anger, perhaps left over from the workplace, that can so easily spill into domestic life if unresolved. A dull red may indicate simmering resentment and so needs handling with tact. A cool clear blue will lower emotional temperatures and a clear green restore loving feelings. A rich brown for joint domestic or practical endeavour can also act as a channel for negative energies.

Business   Scarlet auras directed towards another person, rather than towards a project or worthy cause, do not make for harmonious work relationships for anyone, as inappropriate passion can easily become misdirected anger. It should therefore be countered with a rich yellow for ideas and creativity (which mingled make the integrating orange). Alternatively, a clear but dark blue will introduce the official element that raises thoughts to the level of official matters. A bullying boss with a harsh red aura needs green healing light, plus your own aura should be strengthened with blue as an antidote.

Orange

Love   The colour of self-confidence and independence, so this is not a time to demand constant reassurance that love will last forever. However, the potential warmth and creativity of the interaction is reassurance in itself that all is well. A dull or dirty orange can indicate that one partner is feeling very possessive (maybe because there has been some uncertainty in the relationship), so a clear indigo/deep blue can offer the necessary maturity and detachment to restore the balance.

Family and friends   Clear bright orange is a good robust colour for dealing with friends and family, indicating the balance between the boundaries of self and harmony with others. A very pale orange aura can reveal low self-esteem and fears of losing his or her identity – often there is a harsh red ego in another family member or friend that is acting in a domineering way. This pale aura will be manifest as lack of enthusiasm, self-pity and an inability to forward-plan, so some energising white, gold and yellow may boost confidence.

Business   An excellent aura for work interactions, good for partnerships and for developing individual talents. A dull or murky orange can indicate that someone is feeling very territorial about their rights and responsibilities. In this case a detached clear blue can be an antidote, as can a very rich indigo. In contrast, a pale orange may be manifest by someone who defines his or her worth and identity only in terms of their job description and so may need an energising yellow to melt rigidity.

Yellow

Love   The colour of communication; when the aura is a clear yellow it is a good time to express needs and to make plans for the future that involve movement of any kind, whether travel, house, career changes or new interests. If you crave a period of domestic stability, a little golden brown may slow this winged messenger. However, a dull yellow aura can indicate jealousy and muddied yellow secrets – this is also the colour of the trickster gods. The natural antidote violet will inject integrity, but some clear white light may clarify matters and get positive energies moving.

Family and friends   A buttercup yellow aura typifies modern family life, with every minute taken up with activity and constant electronic communication with mobile phones, faxes and e-mail, especially if there are teenagers buzzing around. Any purple, and especially the gentler hues, will calm down the tendency to hyperactivity. Where there are sibling rivalries or inter-generational conflicts, there may be some murkiness around interactions and here a powerful violet will restore spirituality.

Business   Not a work scene where the grass will grow, and there may be a strong competitive edge between colleagues that can make for a harsh yellow in interactions. Rich blue and violet will help to maintain integrity and encourage responsibility rather than personal rivalry.

Green

Love   This is the colour of true love, and in a clear, rich shade, committed love and fidelity. Combined with concern for the natural world and a respect for all people and creatures, this is love that harms none, but enriches all those it touches. A yellowy-green indicates jealousy that stems from insecurity rather than malice. If these fears are not justified, gentle pink is an auric response that will allay anxiety.

Family and friends   A rich green represents nurturing love and is one to be welcomed in the domestic setting. A murky green indicates possessiveness, but note the direction of any rays as this issue can be very cloudy. Too pale a green can indicate sentimentality and a love that may extend to so many people that those in the immediate circle may feel neglected. This is a case for a dose of the rich brown reality principle, plus some bright clear orange to define personal boundaries, so that the love is not dissipated.

Business   A people-centred workplace. If the aura presented is clear and vibrant, interactions will be positive and colleagues regarded as good friends. However, generally it needs to be balanced by blue or bright yellow to promote more formal relationships necessary for impartial decision-making. A cloudy green aura can indicate that the distinctions between work and social life are blurred, and so there is confusion about roles and appropriate work behaviours.

Turquoise

Love   This colour in the aura of a lover indicates that he or she would die for love; he or she will write beautiful poetry and carve his or her own marriage bed. Any interactions will be fulfilling and enduring. There are no negative connotations.

Family and friends   Again, this aura represents altruism and mature wisdom, even in a young person, and so any interactions will be empowering and fulfilling.

Business   This is a balanced auric colour for mature and honest communication, in which the emphasis is on mutual benefit and problem solving.

Blue

Love   A colour of mature or idealistic love – the marriage of minds and ideas is the aspect that predominates. It is a good colour for long-term commitment and even working together. A harsh blue can indicate a possible power struggle within the relationship or outside interference that is causing friction. A clear pink will defuse the situation, but a positive orange may also be required to assert one's own identity and avoid being steamrollered.

Family and friends   A bright blue in the family setting augurs a lively exchange of ideas, but also a strong sense of justice. A dull blue may indicate depression or anxiety, perhaps from work or unrelated matters that may nevertheless need patience and reassurance – the natural antidote colour red may be needed to reaffirm survival instincts and restore vitality.

Business   An ideal auric colour, especially for brainstorming since the emphasis is on breadth of vision and the expansion of possibility. In a job interview, this colour in the interviewer's aura would suggest that career prospects are favourable. Only a harsh blue indicates an autocratic mood and a rigid mind set, so if an employer is in this mood, pink for reconciliation or grey for compromise and a low profile are the best options.

Purple/violet/indigo

Love The stuff of dreams and of spiritual love, perhaps linked in some way with a past life, twin souls, or space together in which to weave dreams and share the true magic of love. A very pale purple can indicate unworldliness and perhaps unrealistic expectations – this aura can indicate that the possessor puts partners on a pedestal and may just as easily become disillusioned. Therefore this is an aura to counter with some brilliant orange and yellow to give substance to the interaction.

Family and friends In the family, this aura indicates spiritual values and an emphasis on slower cycles of time and connections – but there may be frustration if you are trying to talk about the mortgage or to pin down the other person to solve practical problems. A rich golden brown will provide *earthing*. Only when the purple is very dark is there a sense of loneliness and a feeling of being misunderstood and out of step with others. Again, yellow or orange will restore vitality and connection.

Business Surprisingly, this can represent interactions of integrity and originality and be a successful aura for creative ventures and those involved in the New Age. When the purple becomes too pale, drive and incentive may be lacking. Yellow is an instant as well as a natural antidote.

Pink

Love If you are in the mood for poetry, roses and nostalgic movies, this is the perfect auric colour for a lover. Only a real baby doll pink may suggest that the possessor has a problem with maintaining equal relationships and that dependency looms as an issue, if not now then in future interactions.

Family and friends   Pink reflects peace and kindness and a spirituality manifest through caring, personal relationships. If, however, the colour is confined to one family member, the aura of the peace-keeper will almost certainly be pale or dull and streaked with conflicts and emotions absorbed from others. A clear blue for detachment will be needed to break the martyr mode.

Business   Whether the business involves caring for others or not, this aura of calm will permeate the entire workplace. Only a very misty pink indicates that the path of least resistance will take precedence over justice. A bright power red or blue will keep the interaction on track.

Brown

Love   A colour for a practical approach. It is a good time to ask your lover to fix the sink, and he or she may surprise you with some organic vegetables and fruit as a gift. If you want passion, you will need to progress via pink to red. Only if the brown is dull or harsh are less positive qualities present, and you can counter these with silver or purple to introduce a more spiritual and aesthetic note.

Family and friends   Loyalty and reliability are high when a golden brown aura permeates interactions, as well as a welcoming atmosphere wherever the possessor of this aura lives or socialises. However, a dull brown aura around one family member can indicate that he or she is burdened with more than their fair share of chores and practical responsibilities, and may need vibrant orange to restore self-esteem and a rich blue to fight injustice.

Business   Brown indicates good financial acumen but also caution, so schemes involving risk will not be fruitful. Emotions will not be welcomed in work interactions, and if the brown is harsh material considerations may come before people. Green or pink are best for restoring the balance.

Black

Love A strong black aura indicates a period of regeneration and so is not really amenable to any contact apart from reassurance, although healing white may allow some interaction. If the black is very dense, this is a back-off signal that must be accepted.

Family and friends A rich, clear black is the colour of someone who accepts the frailty of others. A metallic harsh black is the sign of a psychic vampire, so beware of spending too much energy on friends or family members who offload problems, leaving you depressed and themselves energised.

Business Not a good aura for open dealings, so if possible this is a person of whom to steer clear.

Grey

Love A good aura to see in a lover if there are delicate negotiations or potential conflicts as he or she is willing to listen to your point of view and to compromise. However, a pale grey means that decisions or commitments will be very difficult to extract, unless you can inject the interaction with a rich blue, and even some survival red.

Family and friends This is not an aura to cause emotional shockwaves and so can make for tranquil interactions and an undemanding companion. Only a murky grey indicates matters that are being concealed, not necessarily for the best motives. Clear white will encourage frankness.

Business Adaptability and the ability to make things happen unobtrusively can be advantageous, but for incisive decisions an infusion of orange or yellow may be necessary.

Silver

Love As the colour of the Moon and the Moon Goddesses, silver is the colour of lovers, and so interactions will be romantic, mystic and bring connection on a psychic level – you probably experience telepathy if this aura frequently appears. Sexuality may be awakening or perhaps rekindled in the relationship, especially if there are stars in the aura – sometimes a sign of imminent conception.

Family and friends   The aura of imagination and an ability to see beauty and magic everywhere, this is a communication based on intuitive awareness rather than words. Sharing secret dreams can lead to a level of spiritual intimacy.

Business   Not an aura conducive to business affairs, as it can too often represent illusion and promises that cannot be fulfilled.

Gold

Love   Seen rarely in auras, this would indicate a visionary person whose lover would need to follow and share the dangers and uncertainty of trying to change the world. This person will never be less than noble.

Family and friends   No domestic setting would be enough, so prepare for a nomadic life, but one in which a rich vista of experience will be shared. There is little point in trying to modify this aura.

Business   Unless the gold is harsh, this aura belongs to one who will go far, so trust him or her with your investments and be prepared to risk all to gain a great deal.

CHANGING THE AURIC BALANCE OF AN INTERACTION

Modifying your own aura

This involves presenting either an antidote or complementary colour to that of your partner, and this is true whether you are spending an evening with a lover or meeting your bank manager to negotiate a loan. For this reason some spiritual groups and Wiccans hold visualisation rituals to create an aura of peace, healing or to raise a cone of power, and this collective auric power can have a positive effect on the environment. If you are dealing with a group of people, it will take longer and more effort to improve the aura, especially after a quarrel.

For example, if you can offer a softer initial aura in a confrontation, perhaps pink for reconciliation or rich brown for practical proposals, then you can defuse potential opposition. If you need to persuade the other person to accept a new idea or cut through formalities, a clear logical blue or bright yellow should get communication going. Practise with those around you until you've got the idea.

Strengthening your aura

If you are faced with consistent hostility, challenges to your identity and competence, or family members are draining your energy and disturbing your peace of mind by their quarrels or indecision, it is important to strengthen your aura, which may involve using the antidote colour to their own or a stronger colour to assert your identity. Orange is good for self-esteem, red for courage, white for pure energy, blue for necessary detachment and to invoke justice, turquoise for mature wisdom, yellow for logic and clear communication, silver for fertility and a touch of magic – and if the situation is really dire, gold to inspire and uplift you.

METHODS OF CHANNELLING AURIC COLOURS

A natural source of colour, for example sunshine or flowers, contains *prana* or the 'life force' and so is more readily absorbed and fast-acting. Raw or unprocessed food and drink also contain *prana* to a high concentration, and eating different coloured foods follows the ancient magical tradition of absorbing energies.

A related method of taking in specific colours is to drink

water in which an appropriately coloured crystal has been soaked for twenty-four hours, or which has been left in sunlight, its container covered with Perspex of the required colour (also see Chapter 8). You can also buy specially coloured stained glass bottles and keep spring water in them in your refrigerator, which will serve the same purpose.

Crystals are themselves another excellent source of natural colour and you can create a rainbow of small crystals at home or in a dish in your workspace, to act as a focus for absorbing coloured light. Necklaces with a variety of coloured crystals are especially useful since you can touch the appropriate colours while continuing to talk or work. Coloured candles are another potent source of coloured light.

Colour from food and drink

A relatively small amount of food and drink will give you instant colour. As you eat or drink, feel the colour suffusing your body and enveloping you in a coloured bubble. *Feel* the colour, warm and vibrant or gentle and soothing flowing through you like waves. If you cannot have a variety of foods, small fruit sweets, as long as they are made from pure fruit and honey, offer an instant source of colour. You can add your crystal water to any drink.

WHITE	Milk, eggs, naturally bleached bread, white rice.
RED	Apples, redcurrants, strawberries, red peppers.
ORANGE	Carrots, oranges, melons, pumpkins.
YELLOW	Bananas, sweetcorn, grapefruit, yellow peppers.
GREEN	Cucumber, pears, lettuce, spinach, grapes.
BLUE	Plums, blueberries, damsons.
PURPLE/VIOLET/ INDIGO	Blackcurrants, grapes, aubergines.
PINK	Pink grapefruit, pink melon, raspberries.
BROWN	Nuts, raisins, potatoes.

Colour visualisation

Most methods of colour visualisation require time and a quiet place, whether you are using flowers, crystals or coloured candles as a focus for absorbing coloured energies. These are a good method for aura healing or cleansing when you do have plenty of time; however you can create a storehouse of colour within yourself to be activated in a moment by a short-cut key word or action. In this way you can bring the necessary colour to the fore from your full psychic storehouse.

Using flowers – breathing in the colour

Flowers, a source of colour rich in *prana,* provide a wonderful focus for colour breathing exercises since they are still filled with living energy. Work with each of the colours in turn, using any flower or shrub of the appropriate colour. Examples include:

WHITE	Madonna lily, snowdrop, lily of the valley.
RED	Poinsettia, rose, carnation, tulip.
ORANGE	Tiger lily, chrysanthemum, marigold.
YELLOW	Sunflower, primrose, daffodil.
GREEN	Evergreens of all kinds, palms, yucca, fern.
BLUE	Bluebell, forget-me-not, hyacinth.
PURPLE/VIOLET/ INDIGO	Iris, violet, lilac.
PINK	Rose, carnations, cherry blossoms.
BROWN	Chrysanthemums, wallflowers, asters.

Substitute any favourites, or those that grow naturally in your own area. You may decide to cultivate a coloured plant collection or to make a rainbow flowerbed in your garden or terrace.

Exercise: Flower visualisation

- *Find a place where you will not be disturbed, and sit in a comfortable position with the top of the flower at eye level so that you can touch it with your outstretched hand.*

- *Take a deep breath slowly in through your nose, touching the flower briefly to make a connection.*

- *Absorb the fragrance and colour of the flower, hold the flower breath for a second or two, and release it through your mouth. Let any negativity flow out, replaced by the living flower essence.*

- *Visualise a bright flower bud of light, the same colour and shade as the flower, spiralling upwards through your body from the base of your spine.*

- *Let the inner flower slowly blossom from the original point, filled with the colour of the living flower.*

- *Keep breathing and absorbing colour from the flower.*

- *When you feel that the colour has reached the crown of your head, see it radiating upwards in rays to the sun and pure white or golden light flowing down and through your body, surrounding it, mingling within your body with the colour of the flower.*

- *Slowly let the inner flower in your spine close and the light will withdraw back to the sun.*

- *At this point, create your psychic short-cut. For example, if you are working with a red rose, touch it once more and say out loud or silently:* 'Whenever I touch/see a red flower, its colour power will flow into me.'

- *Recreate a colour empowerment for each hue. Thereafter, when you need a particular colour, you can touch a flower and invoke its colour energies instantly.*

ABSORBING NATURAL LIGHT AND DARKNESS

White and gold can be absorbed from sunshine and silver from moonlight; grey from mist and rain; red, orange, pink and yellow from sunrise and sunset; creative black from a moonless and starless night. These need no special mantras or methods of absorption.

Open yourself to these natural sources of auric colour and power and for each create a symbol that you can carry that will invoke the energies within you, a gold ring or necklace for the sun, a silver charm for the moon, a tiny grey and black feather kept in a tiny bag with the charm. As you touch them, the moving energies of the colour will permeate you.

You can also absorb blue from the sky, green from the grass, green and grey from a turbulent sea. So powerful are these natural sources of colour that you need only picture the clear blue sky or the golden sunshine, feel the warmth, hear the birds, and the colours are evoked from your inner store.

ABSORBING CRYSTAL COLOUR

In Chapter 3 I listed crystals and gems that contained the power of each colour. These are an especially portable source of colour, and because of their immense variety of hue and their living energies, most will instantly offer you a boost of a particular colour.

Hold the crystal of the colour and shade you require and see in your mind's eye the colour rising up and flowing around your outline, permeating every pore until your whole body vibrates with the brilliant or gentle shade. Now let the colour rise so that it forms a halo round your head. If you look in a mirror you may see the auric glow of the input colour around your head or a faint white radiance. If there is no mirror, visualise the radiance.

If you use very small crystals, carry them in a bag with you, or as suggested, keep a dish in your home or workplace. An interesting observation I have made is that the other person will invariably pick up and hold not his or her current predominant mood colour, but a crystal of the antidote or complementary colour.

CANDLES

If meeting with a lover in the evening, it is relatively easy to light an appropriately coloured candle when she or he enters the room. Where possible use beeswax or candles in which the colour penetrates all the way through. As with crystals you can either work with the main rainbow colours or with shades and colour mixes to strengthen these auric hues.

You can use the same method of colour breathing that you did with crystals and flowers, breathing in the colour and letting any darkness from your own aura be exhaled. Once again, create psychic short-cuts to the specific coloured energies. These can be set up as you extinguish the candle and visualise a crescendo of colour circling the candle and enveloping you. As you blow or snuff out the candle, say or think a simple mantra, for example *'Power of gold, candle bright, fill my aura with your light'*. When you need the colour, visualise the sphere of light and repeat the mantra silently.

MUSICAL NOTES

The ancients wrote about the harmony of the spheres, and traditionally each colour of the rainbow is associated with a musical note that vibrates at the same frequency. For the main rainbow colours, hum quietly, sing or strike the note on a piano or guitar while visualising the colour and singing its name at that pitch.

Red	Orange	Yellow	Green	Blue	Indigo	Violet
Middle C	D	E	F	G	A	B

Exercise: Creating an aura web for understanding the dynamics of a group

- *Observe a group of people you know well either in a social or work setting. See whose aura is the brightest and the extent of its rays.*

- *Note the people to whom the main aura is making a connection and see whether the rays are proceeding in both directions.*

- *Plot the position on paper by drawing a circle to represent the person and colouring in the shade or shades of the aura and the bi-directional rays. Mark in the rays that are travelling to or from the focus aura but are not being reciprocated.*

- *Look at the next brightest aura and plot the connections in the same way.*

- *Continue until you have inter-connected the auras of everyone, although you may find, even in a group, that one person has no connections at all, or sends out auric colours but receives none in return.*

- *Analyse the individual auras first by colour, then by the influences they exert and the ways they are influenced. See who is constantly sending out rays, who receives many energies and whether energies are sent out in equal proportion.*

- *Note rays that move towards an aura but do not reach it – the person may be operating psychic protection. Is there a psychic vampire who sucks energies from others into a dark aura?*

- *You can analyse this in as much or as little detail as you wish, assessing personalities from the predominant auras, working out inter-connections that may in some instances prove surprising.*

- *This is a good exercise to carry out in an unfamiliar setting that will be of importance to you, for example a new workplace or your lover's extended family.*

Chapter 6

Auras and Levels

As you work with auras, you may become aware that the predominant auric colour is a mist through which other colours are faintly visible. It is rather like looking down from a plane, through breaks in the clouds, at houses, trees and roads far below. The view is subject to the variables of the plane's motion, the changing face of the ground as cars move along the roads and lights come on or are switched off, as well as the individual perceptual system that determines what is registered by the mind and what is overlooked.

In the same way, the constantly changing and interacting auras of perceiver and perceived prevent there being a single objective truth about the composition of the aura. Rather, there are different theoretical models – ways of explaining and describing spiritual concepts in material terms. The framework of the model that is used to conceptualise the aura in itself determines the features of the aura studied and the divisions that are imposed upon the swirling bands of colour.

You might find it worthwhile to spend some time drawing up your own framework. Then read what I have written, as well as some of the books I suggest and any other material you can find on auras, and see how those ideas accord with your own explorations.

It has been hypothesised that the aura has between three and eleven levels, also known as layers or bodies. The most popular view is of seven layers, to correspond to the seven main chakra or psychic level energy points throughout the body, although again there is great disagreement as to the number and functions of the chakras.

The aura is energised by the life force and is a manifestation of the coloured patterns of these energies as the life force flows through or is blocked in the various levels of a person's body and spirit. The life force itself is drawn from the earth through the feet, and from the cosmos into the crown of the head. The darker earth energies rise and interact with the higher light energies that descend through the chakra points, each of which generates a different kind and intensity of energy that can appear as a different colour. The chakra energies are believed to interact to create the predominant auric colour.

If you look at images of human auras taken with Kirlian or Kilner techniques, you generally see a haze of colours as the different strands intermingle. Some clairvoyants have described the aura in terms of hoops of colour around the body, others as distinct bands, like the rainbow itself.

However these colours are perceived, many researchers believe the layers, levels or auric bodies are not separate, but are different depths of the same spirit or *etheric* body. The term *etheric* can be confusing because it is also used to describe the innermost and densest level, seen close to the body as grey or silver wisp. It is this spirit body that is said to travel astrally, and on death to live on to form the enduring eternal self. So in this sense your aura reflects your essential self. The more spiritually evolved a person, the easier is temporary detachment from the physical body, for example in out of body experiences.

Emanuel Swedenborg, the 18th-century scientist, Christian mystic and visionary, believed that all people are born to become angels, whatever their religion. If they choose the path of virtue, they can continue on an angelic path after death. He said that every angel remains fully human until eternity but in a more beautiful and perfected form – of the astral or etheric body. So it may be that we all have the potential to develop the aura of a wise teacher or spiritual being; as we evolve spiritually, so our aura operates on higher levels of vibrations.

I struggled with the idea of each level being one and the same when I first studied auras. But in scientific as well as spiritual terms it makes sense that each level occupies the same space, although the range of the higher levels extends further and so it appears that the purple or spirit aura is distant from the physical body. And of course all these layers are contained within, though extend beyond, the physical body, which can also be perceived in terms of the rainbow rays that pervade it, and so the body itself can be seen as a rainbow. It is rather like a Russian nest of dolls, except that you cannot separate them as individual entities.

Holistic medicine and, increasingly, conventional medical practices are recognising the inter-connectedness between an individual's physical, emotional and spiritual wellbeing. Because the spirit body is less dense than the physical body it will reflect changes to health or harmony before they are recognised by or are manifested in physical ways in the conscious mind and body. Therefore, the aura is a good early warning system, not only of stress or potential illness, but also of opportunities and influences from all levels of experience, not least the cosmos. Because the different colours are associated with various parts of the mind and body, darkness or murky colours can pinpoint potential areas of dis-ease (see Chapter 8)

Meditation or visualisation is a good way to perceive the seven levels. The following is a very visual way of exploring the concept.

Exercise: Perceiving the seven auric bodies

- *Sit in front of a wide-angled mirror – a free-standing full-length looking glass is ideal – having arranged behind you seven candles in a diagonal line so that they can all be seen in the mirror.*

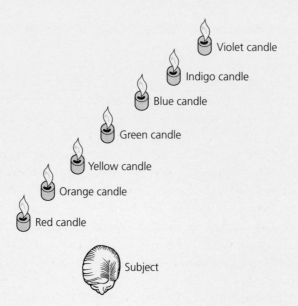

Violet candle

Indigo candle

Blue candle

Green candle

Yellow candle

Orange candle

Red candle

Subject

Mirror

- *First light a red candle behind and slightly to the side of you, then beyond that an orange candle, then in order yellow, green, blue, indigo and violet.*

- *When you can see the candles in a pathway, switch off all other lights and focus first on the red candle. See its rays as a hoop of colour encircling you and visualise the red as a swirling colour combining with your own red auric energies. For each colour you may experience different emotions and sensations.*

- *Continue to focus on each of the colours in turn so that you add to the colour bands whirling round you until all seven send rays upwards to combine as a white halo (the synthesis of the seven colours) above your head.*

- *Sit for a while in the candlelight to strengthen your own aura, leaving you energised but calm.*

- *Let the candles burn through in a safe place.*

- *Whenever you need to study your own auric levels or those*

> *of someone else and find it difficult, recall in your mind the candles.*
>
> • *Repeat the ritual about once a month to keep your aura healthy and to strengthen your auric vision.*

The first auric level in this system is the *Etheric Layer*. In the early stages the first thing you identified was the visible part of the *etheric* or *spirit body* a few centimetres from the skin. As long as you are alive, the aura never completely disappears. But this etheric layer marks the limits of the naturally contracted aura – it is possible to draw the aura in even further when you are suppressing your auric signals deliberately which you will learn to do as a form of psychic protection.

This etheric body is also the only level you might see in someone who is totally exhausted, ill or depressed – any other colours would be so pale and dull as to be almost imperceptible.

As the most dense layer of the spirit body, with the lowest vibrations and closest to the physical body, it especially reflects the physical condition of the whole body. When all is well it may be seen as silver, but as you begin to perceive layers and it expands, it merges into red. Here, survival instincts and the fight or flight mechanism operate along with instincts and physical reactions, such as basic anger or even lust.

The second layer is the *Emotional Body*. This is concerned with emotions, both within ourselves and those we experience when we come into contact with other people; issues of self-esteem, identity and the messages we are given about our worth and attractiveness that filter, sometimes incorrectly, from those around us. It refers to our emotional reactions, as opposed to the higher interactions of the fourth level, and our desires for love, sex, success, even for food or alcohol as an emotional prop. The emotional layer is usually seen as a swirling mass of energy about the body. It is not as clearly defined as the etheric layer. In fact, each successive layer becomes less and less structured.

Its colour begins in the clearer reds and, as it expands, its pure colour is orange. This is the level most subject to change with emotion and where the predominant mood aura will often be seen in earlier aura work, for it will change colour according to events and stress stimuli

The third auric level, the *Mental Layer*, is the layer of thought and ideas, where concepts are fashioned into reality. Here orange merges into pure yellow, and this too is a level that can be affected by everyday interactions and so can merge with the *Emotional Level* to create the predominant mood aura, though it represents a more measured response than pure feelings. It is in this layer that thought and ideas actually become reality.

The fourth auric level, the *Astral Layer*, marks the division between the physical and mental layers and the higher levels of spirit. It is concerned with interaction between people and is the layer of love and of relationships. Emotional bonds are formed on this layer as the colour moves from golden yellow to a pure green glow. Relationship issues on this level can also affect the mood aura.

The fifth auric layer, the *Etheric Template*, is a copy of the physical body on a higher level. It is the master copy on which the *Etheric Body* models itself and green becomes blue, blending in an integrated person as turquoise. It is the level at which the mood and emotions become spiritually and globally focused.

The sixth auric layer forms the *Celestial Body*, the body of emotional level on the spiritual plane. Through this layer we are able to commune personally with the Cosmos and with other dimensions, whether they are perceived as Spirit Guides, Angelic Beings or the Higher Self. It is the level of unconditional love and trust. Here, blue merges with indigo.

The seventh and highest auric layer, the *Ketheric Template*, is also known as the *Causal Body*. This is the highest layer of the spiritual level. Through this layer we can become one with the cosmos, with pure spirit or Divinity. It is akin to Nirvana or merging with the Universal Spirit. This is white or gold.

Exercise: Making a complex auragram

You have already created a simple auragram. Now you are going to make a more complex auragram of the kind that will help in more advanced interpretation and in healing work. To study an aura in this depth, you will need time and patience, not least to discuss the implications with the subject as part of a divinatory or health reading, and then to offer cleansing, energising or healing. So use this auragram as a basis for an intuitive discussion about your subject's life and aspirations.

You can use a slower method of observation, as suggested in Chapter 2, although by now the impressions will probably form spontaneously.

As before, you can either photocopy or scan the diagram on page 95 to create your own auragram. Use a cream- or grey-coloured paper so that the different colours show clearly. As with a true rainbow, colours will merge between layers, and where there is overlap you may get different shades and combination colours. A child is the best subject of all, but should be one you know well and who trusts you. Let the child see you with paper and paints.

This time you will have nine circles (see page 95).

- *As with the simpler form of auragram, the innermost circle represents the* personal or root aura. *With children what you see is what there is, for they are totally open psychically and have no need to hide anything. With adults, you may need to wait until your subject is relaxed; a cup of tea before the reading and a general exchange of pleasantries will evoke this colour. But if the person is very nervous, you may need to build this up from the other layers later. During transition periods in a person's life, this circle may contain streaks of the emerging colour.*

- *The second circle represents the mood aura you may have glimpsed as the person entered the room. As you start to talk in greater depth about any concerns, you may see the predominant colour change. Note both as two separate bands in this circle. Talking time is very important in in-depth aura work, especially if you do not know the person well.*

- *Any stars, jagged lines of darkness or dark spots you can record in the appropriate circle, whether an inner or outer circle. You have now created the overall picture and so can break down the aura into levels.*

- *You are now going to colour in the third circle to represent the etheric body. Colour exactly what you see. As you work outwards, you may, for example, see that the emotional body is suffused with green rather than orange – pure love is guiding and overriding desires. Equally, the fourth level may be flooded with the lower emotional body orange, or even red if food or sex has been confused or substituted for love or approval. Sometimes, if one of the auric levels is particularly strong, it may suffuse the others.*

  In practice, few auragrams are filled in much beyond the fifth or astral level unless the person is very spiritually evolved – even then the sixth layer may be quite ethereal – so do not think that it is your imperfect interpretation.

- *When you are finished, show the auragram to the person with whom you are working. If this is a child, he or she will understand the colours instinctively. With an adult, explain colour meanings, but allow the person to draw conclusions. This is where learning ends and intuition takes over and the finest aura readers will use the auragram to explore not only the challenges but the possibilities inherent in each colour.*

- *Whether used as a divinatory or diagnostic tool the aura-gram should always be given the most positive interpretation and any problems seen as opportunities for change and happier times.*

AURAGRAMS AND DIVINATION

Practise with different people and before long you will find that your auragram is as accurate a form of divination both for yourself and for others as a Tarot reading or astrological chart. Keep a note of your readings for yourself and others, which you should do no more frequently than monthly, except at times of great change or challenge. Over a period of a year you will be amazed at how your own aura has evolved; the outer layers will become increasingly bright and clear as you use the art for others as well as yourself.

AURIC LEVELS AND CHAKRAS

Chakras are believed to be the psychic vortexes through which energy flows from the cosmos and Earth, via the etheric or spirit body, to the physical body. Each of the seven main chakras corresponds to and energises one of the auric levels of the spirit body, as well as a particular area of the physical body. So each chakra radiates its particular colour both within and as a halo around the body. Because chakras exist on the psychic rather than physical level, like the aura itself, they cannot be seen or measured physically.

Most traditions locate chakras vertically along the axis of the body, either on or just in front of the backbone; however they are linked with and take their name from locations on the front of the body, such as the navel, heart, throat and brow. Each chakra level is joined to the next by points or tips, called the roots or hearts of the chakra.

When a particular auric colour appears to dominate auras you know that the corresponding chakra is providing the main energy input. As you read through the following pages you will see how closely the chakra associations are entwined with the different levels of the aura.

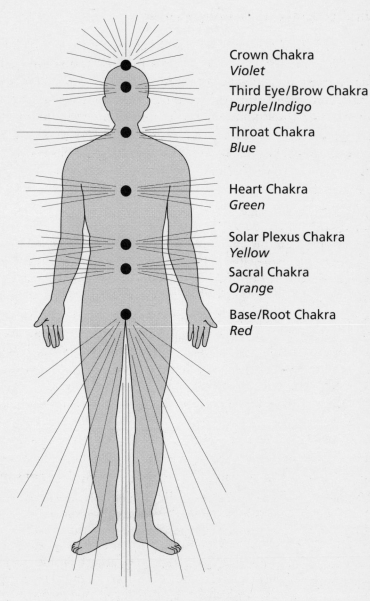

Crown Chakra
Violet

Third Eye/Brow Chakra
Purple/Indigo

Throat Chakra
Blue

Heart Chakra
Green

Solar Plexus Chakra
Yellow

Sacral Chakra
Orange

Base/Root Chakra
Red

The Chakra System

The Seven Major Chakras

Chakra	Colour	Position
Root or Base Chakra or Maladhara	**Red** – rules the first *Etheric* layer of the spirit body and is associated with physical functioning, basic instincts and the five physical senses.	At the base of the spine and linked with the legs, feet, skeleton and the large intestine.
The Sacral Chakra or Svadisthana	**Orange** – rules the second *Emotional* layer of the aura and is associated with spontaneous feelings and urges rather than directed emotions (which reside in the fourth chakra/level of the aura) and with self-esteem and the emerging self-identity.	Seated in the reproductive system and linked with fertility, it also focuses on different aspects of comfort or satisfaction, such as eating, drinking and sexuality and controls the blood, reproductive system, kidneys, circulation and bladder.
The Solar Plexus or Manipura	**Yellow** – rules the third *Mental* level of the aura and is associated with the conscious mind, logic and mental power and control, and also astral travel, as this is the first level of awareness at which the spirit body can temporarily detach itself.	Seated just below the navel, it controls digestion, the liver, spleen, stomach and small intestine. It is said to absorb the life force or *prana* from living food such as fruit, vegetables and seeds.

Chakra	Colour	Position
The Heart Chakra or Anahata	**Green** – rules the fourth *Astral* layer of the aura and is associated with relationships and with emotional stability and harmony within the self as well as with others.	Situated in the centre of the chest, its energies radiating over heart, lungs, breasts and over the arms and hands which hold others in love.
The Throat Chakra or Vishuddha	**Blue** – rules the fifth *Etheric Template* of the aura and is associated with communication and idealism, the synthesis of emotion and thought.	Situated close to the Adam's apple in the centre of the neck. Controls the throat, speech organs, thyroid gland, neck, shoulders and the passages that run up to the ears.
The Third Eye, Brow Chakra or Savikalpa Samadhi	**Purple/indigo** – rules the sixth *Celestial* level of the aura and is associated with unconscious wisdom and psychic powers, especially clairvoyance, but also clairaudience and mediumistic abilities.	Situated just above the bridge of the nose in the centre of the brow and controls the eyes, ears and both hemispheres of the brain.
The Crown Chakra or Nirvakelpa Samadhi	**Violet** merging with white light pouring in from the cosmos. Rules the seventh level, the *Ketheric Template* or *Causal Body*.	Situated at the top of the head in the centre and rules the brain, body and psyche, growth and physical, mental and spiritual well-being.

Exercise: Connecting the Auric and Chakra Energies

Each chakra/auric level has an associated fragrance that can be evoked either in incense or as an oil. In the section on cleansing the aura (pages 103–4), I describe the Native North American method of smudging to cleanse the whole aura. However, by burning a specific auric/chakra fragrance, you can increase the energies flowing from that particular chakra.

The auras and chakras and their corresponding fragrances:

Chakra/Auric Level	Fragrance
Crown Chakra/Ketheric Template	Bergamot, frankincense, sandalwood
Brow Chakra/Celestial Level	Geranium, myrrh, violet
Throat Chakra/Etheric Template	Eucalyptus, lemongrass, peppermint
Heart Chakra/Astral Layer	Chamomile, lavender, rose
Solar Plexus Chakra/Mental Level	Lemon, pine, sage
Sacral Chakra/Emotional Level	Orange, jasmine, ylang-ylang
Root Chakra/Etheric Level	Basil, patchouli, tea tree

Therefore, if you knew that you needed clear thought and logic, you would burn a cleansing Solar Plexus fragrance, for example lemon to stimulate the faculties of the mental layer of the aura. But if you wanted to increase the general transference of energy throughout the entire aura, you could stimulate the chakras by encircling yourself with the incenses for all seven chakras.

- *Make sure the incenses are in a deep upright container at a safe distance from yourself and any fabrics.*

- *Lie on the floor on cushions or on a sofa or bed and to the north of you place a jar containing a Crown Chakra incense stick such as frankincense.*

- *At brow level on either side of you place a Brow Chakra incense and so on with the appropriate incense on both sides of your body level with your throat, heart, navel, womb or genitals and finally to the south a single Root Chakra incense at your feet.*

- *Visualise the smoke as the different colours swirling in bands both within and beyond your body in the auric field around you.*

- *Visualise energies spiralling upwards and downwards, converging and filling you with radiant colour. See your body as a rainbow.*

- *Wait until the incense has burned through and use the time to weave dreams and allow images and sounds to form that may speak of events to come or possible pathways you might follow.*

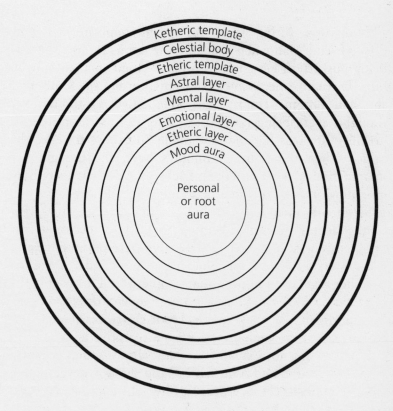

Ketheric template
Celestial body
Etheric template
Astral layer
Mental layer
Emotional layer
Etheric layer
Mood aura

Personal
or root
aura

A more complex auragram

Chapter 7

WORKING WITH THE AURA FOR PROTECTION, HEALTH AND HARMONY

Sarah was sitting in a restaurant opposite her new boyfriend Alan when suddenly she felt as though she was being pushed off her chair by a black cloud emanating from him. Thereafter, her skin began to prickle and she found that she had become clumsy and tongue-tied as though her thoughts were being tangled. So intense was the feeling of hostility towards her that she made an excuse to leave the table. When she returned minutes later, she thought her imagination had been playing tricks as Alan was incredibly charming and relaxed and the evening light-hearted.

Sarah continued to have similar panic attacks, but a visit to the doctor proved unhelpful. Sarah told me about her apparently irrational feelings while we were rehearsing for a TV show. Sarah had a very changeable aura, and as I worked with her regularly I noticed that people would invariably tell her their problems and that her aura would darken and theirs become lighter as they spoke. From this I concluded, not surprisingly, that she had a very open receptive aura.

But that did not explain the panic attacks, until I had a drink with Sarah and Alan with whom she was developing a close relationship. Very imperceptibly and without warning, Alan's jaw tightened, though he was still smiling. His hand muscles tensed slightly and at this point Sarah began to look pale and distracted, although the conversation was still animated and good-natured. As I looked at Alan it was as though storm clouds were gathering over his head and I realised that what Sarah was picking up was an unconscious psychic attack from Alan. Alan did not seem aware that he was directing negativity towards Sarah, and she also did not realise that with her open aura she was receiving it. Afterwards I asked her to explain what she experienced and she again described the black cloud and the sensation of being pushed off her chair.

After Alan had unloaded his conscious negativity he visibly relaxed. I found out that Alan was a depressive with several failed relationships for apparently trivial reasons. It may have been that something in the conversation unwittingly triggered off bad memories for Alan at a very deep level; that was a complex issue that Alan might or might not at some time decide to tackle. But since Sarah was besotted, it was a question of her learning to protect her aura as she was picking up negativity, not only from Alan, but from everyone she met whose problems she absorbed.

Your aura is the reception area for all interactions and energies, positive and negative, from the external world, that are unconsciously as well as consciously projected. It is therefore important to keep your auric field protected and cleansed. I talk about aura cleansing later in the chapter, but if you can filter out stresses and the anxieties or anger of others, you can reduce the causes and consequences of auric imbalance.

In a sense, every positive ritual you carry out affects your aura, and work specifically focused on strengthening your personal auric field and cleansing it of negativity automatically brings positive results in every aspect of your life, for example in terms of clear, impartial thinking and less extreme emotional reactions to minor setbacks and challenges.

AURIC PROTECTION

As you work with auras you become more receptive to the energy fields around you, and especially if you are healing someone's aura, you can become overwhelmed by their energies. You need to protect your own aura in advance.

However, there are times when it is not possible to prepare yourself, for example when a manager, client or colleague storms into your work area seeking confrontation, when you receive an angry phone call or are aware of a hostile or negative atmosphere when you enter a new place. Or it may be that an interfering relation or neighbour invades your personal space with intrusive though not hostile questioning, or wants to offload problems rather than seek creative solutions. Even the constant chatter of children or a friend or colleague when you are trying to work can tangle your aura of harmony.

When you have time to prepare for healing work or an interaction you know may be difficult, it can be empowering to spend a few minutes creating a protective aura. But it is also possible to invoke instant protection through establishing a simple signal linked to an earlier auric protection ritual.

I have suggested two methods, the Shield of Gold for times when it is important to stay powerful, and a pink Shield of Harmony for times when the atmosphere is not hostile but unhappy or emotionally draining. The method for creating both is virtually the same and one I have used with variations for other forms of psychic protection.

Exercise: Creating a gold and silver auric shield

Candles are a natural source of auric light, and gold and silver candles combine solar and lunar energies to give you day and night protection. You can carry out this ritual on a sunny day; the extra light from the candles will amplify the natural latent gold and silver energies within your aura. It is especially powerful if you choose a sunny day when the sun and moon are in the sky at the same time – check your diary or the weather section of a newspaper to discover the next rising of the moon during the daytime. The waxing moon is especially good for rising energies.

Work indoors, or in a sheltered spot in a garden, or on a balcony in a pool of light from the sun. You can experiment with different angled lamps to create a supplementary pool of light if the sun is not in the right place or you need to carry out the ritual in the evening.

- *Sitting in the centre of the circle of light, surround yourself (at a safe distance so you will not burn your clothes or skin when you move) with an ellipse or oval of alternate gold and silver candles.*

- *Begin in the south, the direction of the noonday sun, with a gold candle and light your candles in turn clockwise, saying for the gold:*

    'Burn bright, golden light,
    Drive away all danger,
    Protect me as I work and live,
    From false friend and stranger.'

- *As you light the silver candles say:*

    'Burn bright, silver light,
    Enclosing and protecting,
    Keep me calm, safe from harm,
    From dark emotion shielding.'

- *Repeat this or your own mantra of protection over and over until you are surrounded by a complete circle of gold and silver candlelight.*

- *Now turn nine times clockwise within the circle of candles and sunshine, repeating the two invocations, one after the other.*

- *Sit once more within the circle of light and visualise it hardening like a transparent shimmering gold and silver shield above your head, below your feet, and all around you in a sphere. Extend your hands so you can feel its edges.*

- *Now you need to decide on your activation mechanism for times when you cannot light a candle ring – perhaps touching your unseen psychic Third Eye in the position between and just above your physical eyes. As you do so, say:*

  'When I awaken my Third Eye by touching it, I will automatically bring to life my candle circle of personal power and protection.'

- *Blow out your candles anti-clockwise, beginning with the silver one immediately to the right of your southernmost gold candle, so that the last candle alight is the first gold one you ignited. Let the light fade, but know that it is always there to be activated at times of need.*

- *Repeat your candle ritual regularly whenever you feel your auric protection getting weaker.*

Creating a pink shield of harmony

In the previous exercise protection was given against both hostile and non-aggressive attacks that were nevertheless intrusive. This second more gentle mode of protection excludes from your auric field those who may be vulnerable, but would draw energy from you at a time when you have little to spare: the person in the next seat on a crowded train who is desperate to talk when all you want to do is sleep; a child's incessant demands on a wet day when you begin to feel irritated, but cannot go out; a lonely neighbour whose regular visits disrupt your schedule. In all these cases you do not want to hurt sensitive feelings, merely reinforce your separate auric space.

This time, use pink candles to make the ellipse shape around yourself.

- *Begin the ritual at dawn, when pink light floods the sky. Face the east, the direction of the rising light.*

- *Light each candle in turn, clockwise, saying as you light each candle:*

  Pink of Morn, healing Dawn
  Enclose me in peace,
  Let the world flow away
  And all intrusion cease.

- *Because this time you want a different signal, touch your heart or your breast bone in the centre of your chest, level with your heart, the seat of the Heart Chakra, and say:*

  'When I awaken my Heart power by touching it, I will automatically bring to life my auric shield of harmony and mutual safe keeping.'

AURIC INVISIBILITY

Auric protection is also of value in making yourself less visible in situations or places in which you are vulnerable. Most ancient invisibility spells relied not on making the physical body disappear, but on lowering a person's profile so that he or she could walk unnoticed in places of potential danger.

In spite of taking precautions, there are times when we may be left to lock up an empty workplace late in the evening; when we have to return to a deserted car park or wait on a station late at night or for a taxi in an area in which there are gangs of drunks or troublemakers.

Such situations can benefit from auric protection, just as much as open attacks of spite. The easiest method is to contract the aura, so that you give off no signals and merge into the background. It is one I have used many times late at night.

Exercise: Withdrawing the aura

The naturally contracted aura, the external part of the spirit body, is no more than a few centimetres from the skin. However, with practice, it is possible to withdraw the aura for short periods so that it is entirely within the physical body.

- *Deliberately quieten your thoughts so that your aura is not fuelled by emotion, rather like putting a car in neutral gear.*
- *If you are in a dark place, breathe in the gentle blackness through your nose and hold your breath for a count of one and two and three.*

101

- *As you do so, contract and tense your muscles, feeling the aura move closer to your skin.*
- *Breathe out all doubts and fears as mingled red and dull green light.*
- *If there are lights or you find it difficult to quell your fear, close your eyes and imagine a starlit sky, and the stars fading one by one to leave you cloaked in dark soft velvet. For this is not terrifying blackness, but the all-embracing mantle of Mother Earth at midnight, what the Chinese call pure Yin, the seamless cloak that envelops all.*
- *Continue until you feel the gentle tug as your aura is pulled level with your skin, like an umbrella folding or a tent being pushed back into its bag.*
- *When it is safe again, simply exhale the darkness as pure single breaths and inhale white or golden visualised light.*
- *Practise this in bed at night as a good way of relaxing. When you are asleep your aura automatically expands to embrace the dream world and the astral planes.*

Exercise: Creating an aura of greyness

This is a variation of a method I have described in other books, as I find it the most effective and easiest form of psychic protection. It is like withdrawing the aura – useful to adopt when you are in a vulnerable position, when travelling, or when in a crowded place if you would like to be left undisturbed. The greyness masks the normal auric signals we emit when we are afraid or anxious. It can also be helpful in new situations and places where you need to study the dynamics of a place before making your presence felt.

There are similarities between this process and making your aura grey, but this is a denser, mistier grey – if you look in a mirror after you have created a cloak of grey, your outline may seem blurred.

- *Sit in a comfortable position and close your eyes.*
- *Visualise the circle of swirling colours around your head*

and body. Gradually slow them right down until the movement is like a flower swaying very gently in a light breeze.

- *Draw in the rays of colour and lights like a flower closing at night.*

- *See now a soft warm mist descending from above and rising from the earth to envelop you in gentle greyness from which you can see out but are less invisible to the external world.*

- *When the danger or potential intrusion has passed, let the mist disperse and your aura unfold once more.*

CLEANSING THE AURA/AURA BALANCING

Even with protection, your aura can become tangled with the negativity or anxieties of others and suffer as a result of pollutants, stress, overwork or junk food and lack of fresh air. Because the ill-effects of these are seen in the aura before they reach the physical body, you can remove them by cleansing the aura and give energy and harmony to your body and mind to replace any negativity.

Though some people prefer to cleanse the aura in the morning, late evening is a good time to remove the day's negativity, so that you will enjoy restful sleep and wake naturally energised. In the morning, balance the colours in your aura, perhaps strengthening any you know will be needed (see page 75).

Exercise: Using water

This exercise can be carried out either in the evening by candlelight or in the morning by the light of dawn. You can obtain sacred water from many of the holy wells that date back thousands of years to the time they were believed to be the entrance to the womb of the Earth Mother, for example the Chalice Well in Glastonbury Water or the Abbess Well in Minster, Kent. If you do not have any sacred water, substitute nine drops of a cleansing and empowering flower essence, such as Glastonbury Thorn Essence, Bach's Cherry Plum, the Deva Flower Elixir Morning Glory or the Findhorn Scottish Primrose.

- *Light pink candles in a safe place in the bathroom. (You may also wish to light candles at dawn if your bathroom has poor natural light.)*
- *Add nine drops of sacred water to your evening bath before you use any oils or bath foam. As you sit in the water, touch each of your chakra points, beginning at the crown of your head, your brow, your throat, heart, navel, womb or genitals and finally the base of your spine and then your left and right foot. The last three are all linked to the Root chakra, but make the sacred nine.*
- *As you touch each chakra point, chant a variation of the ancient cleansing rhyme:*

  'Sorrow, darkness flow from me, from the rivers to the sea.'

- *Then add any oils or bath foam and visualise any darkness from your aura flowing into the bath water.*
- *As you pull out the plug, repeat the chant and watch the auric darkness flowing away.*
- *Shake yourself free of any lingering auric darkness then sit for a few moments in the candlelight, letting the light fill your aura with harmonious energies to replace what you have removed.*

SMUDGING

This can be carried out whenever auric cleansing seems necessary, for example after a particularly negative encounter, an auric interpretation or healing work that has left you feeling exhausted and enervated.

Smudging is a traditional Native American way of cleansing the auric field through the burning of sage, cedar, tobacco and sweet grass, without directly inhaling it. Because tobacco has lost its ceremonial significance and smoking has become a social rather than a ritual activity, modern smudging rituals do not use tobacco. Smudging removes any negative feelings, depression and anxiety and restores a state of harmony, so that healing will occur naturally as positive energies are absorbed.

MAKING AND USING A SMUDGE STICK

Making a smudge stick and using it ritually is remarkably easy. Commercially prepared smudge sticks are sold in New Age stores if you do not wish to make your own.

Use about six or seven 15cm (6in) long sprigs of the fresh herbs. Hold these tightly together and bind them with cotton thread, tying them at every centimetre along their lengths. Leave them to dry for two or three weeks. (If you are pregnant, substitute lavender, pine or eucalyptus as your cleansing herbs.) Light a candle of green or brown for the Earth Mother and hold the smudge stick about 5cm (2in) above the flame until it glows and smoulders, releasing a thin trail of smoke.

Move from the bottom to the top of the body in a clockwise or sunwise direction, making an anti-clockwise circle a few centimetres above the crown to remove negative influences, and then clockwise to add power. As you work, take in the elliptical shape or the aura around your body, especially over the crown of your head.

Carry out this ritual six times for the six cardinal North American directions: north, south, east, west, up and down, seeing darkness leaving the aura and being replaced by golden healing light. Alternatively, follow the traditional method of using a fireproof bowl or deep shell to contain rolled and dried herbs, lit from a taper from the Mother Earth candle.

In this case, use a feather or your hand to waft the smoke all around you or the person whose aura you are cleansing.

Another name for this ceremony is *sweeping medicine*.

Another alternative is to waft incense sticks of the traditional smudging fragrances in front of you, as long as you use solid ones that will not crumble and burn you.

Smudging is also used for general bodily healing as well as alleviating specific illnesses.

THE HERBS

Sage

Sage is, as in many other cultures, a herb of wisdom, and when burned offers protection from all forms of harm and negative feelings in the self and others. The negativity rises into the cosmos to be transformed by the Great Spirit. Because it grows in the desert, sage represents the energies of both the sun or Fire, the south and Earth, the north.

Sweet grass

Sweet grass grows high in the Rocky Mountains, and is called the grass that never dies. It is also found on marshes and near lakes and so combines the power of Air, the east, and Water, the west. Its power lies in its connections with the world of spirit, calling down health and plenty from the benign forces above as it burns.

Cedar

Cedar is a herb of purification, protection and healing and can be used either with the two other substances or as a substitute for sweet grass.

Rosemary or hyssop are also used for smudging, but are not advisable in pregnancy.

Exercise: Using colour breathing for cleansing and balancing the aura

You have already used pranic or colour breathing as a method of absorbing colour from flowers in Chapter 5. Breathing in and exhaling as you visualise the breath as different colours is a method that can be used any time you need energising or calming. You can remove general negativity from the aura by exhaling it as dark, dull or murky colours. You can then balance your aura by introducing lighter, brighter hues.

If you know that you need a specific colour for a situation or interaction during the day ahead, or are aware when you look at your own aura in the mirror that certain colours are missing while others are too harsh or murky, you can add colour or replace the excess colours through pranic breathing. Maybe your aura is flooded with red because of unfair treatment. The moment has passed but your heart is still racing, colour is flushing your cheeks and you cannot settle, even hours later. You could cleanse your aura or you could simply replace the excess colour with its antidote, blue, or a soothing complementary colour such as green.

Colour cleansing and balancing is a good way of beginning a day or relaxing after stress, but you can also use the technique in a modified form, perhaps concentrating on breathing in one or two required colours on a train, in the office or even sitting on a park bench at lunchtime.

* Sit comfortably with your feet touching the floor.
* Take a deep breath through your nose and, as you do so, tense your body by placing your hands behind your head, with your elbows pointing forward, then move your elbows out so they are pointing to the sides and lean your head back gently.
* Breathe out slowly through your mouth, releasing your arms and extending them as widely as possible at shoulder height, stretching like a cat awaking from sleep.

- *Return them to your lap or sides, whichever feels most comfortable.*

- *Breathe in slowly. Hold this breath for a slow count of three (count one and two and three), then exhale slowly through your mouth with a sigh. Do this five or six times. Visualise the air you are inhaling as pure white or golden light, radiating through your body.*

- *Exhale slowly, visualising black mist being expelled, leaving your body lighter and more harmonious.*

- *Slow your breathing a little, visualising golden or white light entering your lungs and spreading throughout your body.*

- *Hold your breath (count one and two and three).*

- *Breathe out slowly, once again expelling the dark mist. Pause then repeat the pattern, each time visualising the dark mist leaving your body, becoming paler as the negativity is expelled.*

Once you are happy with this method you can adapt it to specific colour breathing. Use your exhaled breath to banish negativity and your inhaled colour to introduce calm or energy, according to your needs. The warmer colours – red, yellow and orange – are stimulating and energising for the aura; blue, green and purple, the cooler colours, soothe and gently uplift.

For **instant energy** or **courage**, inhale red and exhale blue.

For **deliberate thought** and **wisdom**, inhale blue and exhale red.

For **confidence**, inhale orange and exhale indigo.

For **significant dreams**, inhale indigo and exhale orange.

For **calm**, inhale green and exhale turquoise. Because green is a neutral colour the need for balancing its energies is usually very subtle. This is why spiritual turquoise is such a good colour to use.

For **spiritual** or **psychic awareness**, inhale turquoise and exhale green.

For **intuition**, inhale violet and exhale yellow.

For **communication** or **learning**, inhale yellow and exhale violet.

For **positivity**, inhale white or gold and exhale black.

When you feel totally balanced and harmonious, and are either ready for action or sleep according to the colours you breathed, stretch and circle your hands around your head and shoulders, feeling the renewed colours either moving slowly and in harmony or whirling with energy and optimism. Look in the mirror and see the colours dance.

Chapter 8

HEALING THE AURAS OF OTHERS

Healing is a gift possessed by everyone, if we trust our innate wisdom to guide our hands. Like all spiritual and psychic powers, you will heal most easily those with whom you have a strong emotional connection, so begin your auric healing work on children, close friends and family. You can also send light to the auras of absent friends and relations. Many professional healers first discovered their abilities while healing a child or partner.

This chapter concentrates mainly on healing others, but if you still sense problems in your own aura after following the cleansing and protective rituals suggested in Chapter 7, at the end of this chapter I outline a very powerful healing method adapted from the Native North American traditions that you can use for yourself, or adapt for others as part of a guided visualisation.

If you do want to develop your healing powers more formally, whether professionally or privately, I have listed several healing organisations in Useful Addresses (page 157) that may be of help.

Aura healing is not a substitute for conventional medical care, and if you or someone close to you has persistent symptoms or acute pain, especially a child or much older person, then either your doctor or qualified alternative practitioner should be consulted. However, even in these cases, healing the aura can augment more formal methods of medicine and is especially valuable in detecting and alleviating potential problems before they manifest as physical symptoms.

As with all psychic work, the key to healing possible health problems manifest in the aura lies in using intuitive powers to interpret the significance in an individual case of dark or dull areas, or even missing areas or colours. Some people can see or sense health, or problems with it, in concentric bands of colour within the body, rising from red/brown around the feet/earth to violet/white at the crown of the head. These bands reflect the colours of the chakras.

Other people detect problems purely in the area of the bio-field beyond the body, the true aura, and may diagnose physical and well as emotional and spiritual problems as holes, dark spots or an area which bulges or seems to disappear. Harsh or dull colours in different areas can also indicate potential problems. If, for example, you detected discoloration around the throat area, or in the astral layer which rules the throat, but the subject was experiencing no symptoms, you would consider this as an early warning of potential throat problems. You might advise the subject to avoid smoke-filled places.

The source of the problem may come from elsewhere. For example, if someone talks of stomach cramps, you may detect darkness or a tear in the astral level indicating that problems with a relationship or giving too much emotionally to others are appearing as tension or tightness in the digestive system. If unresolved, this might develop into a stomach ulcer or general digestive problems. The process is an interactive one. If you mention that there appears to be a misshapen or missing part of the aura, the person may spontaneously talk about overload or unmet needs in one area of their life.

There are no standard formulas for detecting dis-ease or dis-order. The key to successful diagnostic and healing work is to forget what you are supposed to be looking for and trust what you actually sense or see and the images and words that come into your mind as the two auras meet. If you speak from your heart and let your hands (ruled by the Heart chakra) move spontaneously, healing powers will flow – remember those beautiful coloured flares emanating from healers' hands that I mentioned in Chapter 1? Your unique system of diagnosis will evolve naturally as you heal yourself and others.

Exercise: Healing the aura

Any form of healing takes energy, so monitor your own energy levels when healing others; when you are exhausted, it is much easier for you to fall ill. I gave a very sick friend a crystal that was charged with my own health at a time when I was exhausted. Thereafter I suffered six weeks of a very nasty virus to which I had no resistance because I had, with the best intentions, given my health away.

You have already used the separate stages of healing in your aura work – now you can combine them to create a healing ritual.

- *Ask the person you are healing if he or she would feel more relaxed sitting rather than lying down.*
- *Use soft lighting in the form of purple candles with an oil or incense of gentle restorative energies, such as lavender or rose, and perhaps background music of natural sounds. Alternatively, work in the open air on a warm day in a sheltered spot near fragrant flowers. If you are working indoors, have a bowl of fruit and living plants rather than cut flowers to increase the life force. A water feature will also encourage the flow of natural energies.*
- *Allow your psychometric abilities to guide you, and without touching the physical form feel any energy disturbance or imbalance as though within yourself. Take sufficient time to allow impressions to form, but resist the temptation to allow the analytical part of the brain to intrude. Energy blockages, imbalances and negativity feel distinctly different from positive energy. Many people*

describe the sensation of hitting a bad spot as cold, jarring like a painful tooth that suddenly encounters ice.

- First cleanse the aura by removing these energy blockages or disturbances and tangles.

- Next fill any holes or repair any jagged tears with specific colours of energy – or antidote colours in the case of a harsh or murky shade – to restore strength. Energise the whole aura with light and finally seal it.

The closer the darkness or discoloration to the body, the more it is related to the physiological sphere. Some dark areas may penetrate all the layers, indicating perhaps that a spiritual crisis or negativity that has hurt the soul has filtered through to the etheric layer and may either currently or in the future be manifest as headaches or stress-related conditions.

CLEANSING THE AURA

If the aura is clear and there seem to be no problems, you can simply energise it. To cleanse the aura, trace the etheric level of the subject, moving one hand along each side of the body, 5cm away. Move outwards until you encounter a blockage that may seem like tangled thread or hair. Continue until you have identified all the blockages. If you cannot feel anything specific, but sense a general imbalance, the person may be suffering a general energy loss in the aura.

To remove a dark spot, close your cupped hands around the area and gently pull it like a strand of wool from the person being healed. Direct the negative energy down into the Earth, to be transformed to positivity. Grasp a longer jagged dark area between finger and thumb, like a long dark splinter, and cast it into the sky to become a beam of light.

REPAIRING HOLES OR TEARS IN THE AURA

Holes or tears in the aura leak vital energy out of this auric system, leading to fatigue and a tendency to infections.

Gently probe the different levels and see whether you can still feel any holes or tears that did not spontaneously heal during the first stage of cleansing. If you are uncertain, use a crystal pendulum to indicate areas where the aura has worn thin or is torn. The pendulum will spiral anti-clockwise over these places.

To fill an area of the aura, make an arch with your hands around the affected area, or just above the crown of the head, and visualise pure white or golden light pouring from your fingers down the inner energy channels into the area that you have just cleansed. The person being healed may say that they are experiencing gentle warmth. Use slow and regular breathing as you work, breathing in golden *pranic* light from the cosmos and breathing out dark, stale light.

Another effective method, especially if a colour is murky or very pale, is to take a crystal of the appropriate auric colour that needs strengthening or replacing. If the tear or hole spans more than one level, use an amethyst and place it above the tear, circling clockwise over the area. See the crystal releasing fibres of light to fill the gap, and the colour seeping within the aura, enriching and energising it.

If a tear or hole seems deep or is very large, or an area of the aura is missing, surround the person being healed with a circle of small candles of the required auric colour or deep purple. Sit outside the circle and visualise the light entering the crown of the head of the person and radiating through either the specific chakra or every level of the body and beyond for a more general tear. Let the candles burn for a few minutes, then ask the subject to blow them out one by one, letting the light surround and permeate him or her.

ENERGISING AND SEALING THE AURA

Once you have cleansed and repaired the aura, the next stage is to fill it with positive energy. For the best effect, use pure white or golden light, the synthesis of the rainbow colours. As I have said before, a person will absorb the colours and energies he or she needs; the rest will act as a repository for when additional strength is needed.

You can energise and seal the aura using the flares of energy that naturally emanate from your fingertips when you undertake healing work. You can also use this method for energising your own aura by directing the light from your fingers into a circle, rather than outwards to the person being healed. It is also a good method of general psychic protection.

Shake your fingertips until you can feel the energy flowing. Hold your hands about 15cm apart, fingers spread wide open, palms facing each other. Slowly bring your hands together until they almost touch, then draw them apart. Repeat this movement for five or six cycles until you see faint light – you did this when first exploring auric energies.

Now move your hands in the same position, this time rotating your power hand (the one you write with) clockwise and the other anti-clockwise in ever more rapid circles, visualising the light becoming brighter and clearer and creating sparks or rays, in yellow, orange and gold. Circle your hands in the same manner above the person you are healing and see the light entering the aura and forming a golden opaque sphere around the whole person.

If you are energising and sealing your own aura, hold your hands above your head, extending the sparks from your left hand so that they move clockwise and upwards in the shape of the golden sphere around your body, until they join with your right hand. See them forming a golden protective sphere.

After the healing spend some time talking quietly with

your subject, and share a drink or light meal to ground your-
selves once more. When the subject has gone, have a slow
bath using a few drops of peppermint or pine essential oil.
Use a crystal pendulum clockwise over your aura to restore
your own energy levels.

ABSENT HEALING

If a person is absent, visualise him or her sitting in a soft
rainbow light and draw an auragram of the colours you see
or sense, and any holes, tears or darkness, recording whether
they penetrate a number of layers.

This time, hold your crystal pendulum over the auragram
and see where it spirals anti-clockwise to indicate blockages
or tangles. Visualise them in the aura of the absent subject.

Next, circle a crystal of the appropriate colour over the
auragram, concentrating especially on any tears, holes, darkness or discoloration. As you do so, visualise coloured
energies flowing into the actual aura. Once again, if healing
more than one layer use an amethyst.

You can use white clay or a soft flour, oil and water dough
in the shape of a figure to represent the absent person.
Around the form, mould on to the clay figure the first level
of the aura as a long strand of dough, following the shape,
then add strands extending outwards to represent the next
six layers. As you continue to picture the distant aura, create
holes in the clay in places where there is an auric tear. You
can also colour in areas of discoloration and jagged tears on
the model using an indelible marker. With a twig picked from
a healing ash tree or a nut or fruit-bearing tree, gently remove
any areas of darkness or murkiness from the clay figure and
bury them in the Earth, smoothing out and remoulding any
holes.

Circle the head and outermost auric level of the clay figure
with either your pendulum or a clear quartz crystal, once
more visualising the healing light pouring within and

forming a protective sphere all around the body and auric field. Bake the clay or dough figure gently and place it close to greenery for a twenty-four-hour cycle. Keep it wrapped in white silk in a safe place until the person you have tried to heal is well.

HEALING THE AURA USING THE 'BEAUTY WAY'

Native North American peoples frequently talk of the 'Beauty Way', the path they follow through life. Many of their great inspirational figures, for example the White Buffalo Calf Woman, the sacred Creator Woman of the Lakotas, are seen walking along a path of light from the horizon and disappear the same way. Legend has it that White Calf Woman fell from a meteor, and as she began her Earth Walk, she taught sacred ceremonies for restoring balance and healing to both earth and people.

This radiance can be used to give a sudden surge of energy and to restore optimism. It is an excellent antidote for Seasonal Affective Disorder (SAD), whereby the dark days of winter and lack of sunlight bring bouts of depression. The auras of those living in colder countries, where the skies are perpetually grey, are darker and less vibrant than those who live close to the blue Mediterranean.

For this method you need to reflect light on to your head and body as you walk along a path. You could create a path of glass nuggets or tiny crystal beads. Use mirrors and lights and experiment until you have enclosed the whole path in light. Fibre optic lamps are an excellent source of moving light. Use the *pranic* breathing method to absorb light and let it expand from your inner core outwards so that every layer of your aura is energised as you walk.

An alternative technique is to use a natural Beauty Way, a path of light: a beach at Full Moon will offer a pathway of light across the sea, and you can wade out a little way and stand in the golden water. Alternatively, go to a formal garden with paths laid out between flowers and wait until there is a long straight path bathed in sunlight with the borders shaded. An urban park or square will serve just as well. You will rapidly become expert at finding likely spots.

Let the gold enter your every pore and flood through you so that your whole body is warmed by the radiance.

Exercise: Restoring the harmony to a special place or to the planet

As a result of pollution and deforestation, global warming has damaged the planet's aura, while places of natural beauty can readily lose their natural life force if they are near electricity pylons or a nuclear power station, or surrounding trees have been cut down and replaced with roads and houses. Light pollution, the lights generated by towns, prevents us from seeing stars in the aura of the sky.

The following ritual is one used by Inuit shamans who untangle the aura of Sedna the Sea Mother who controls life and fertility, so releasing the fishes and sea animals into the sea. This is an especially potent ritual for polluted seas and rivers, but can help anywhere that the natural aura of sky and earth has become clogged with industrialisation. This ritual not only releases the energies of natural places but can also heal your personal aura if you have been overwhelmed by the problems or conflicts of others, or the energies around you have become stagnant.

- *Begin by pouring into the sea, a flowing source of water, or a hole on barren land, nine drops of a restorative flower essence. I use the Glastonbury Thorn. Also potent is the Alaskan Flower Remedy, the Balsam Poplar (Populus Balsamifera) that removes energy blockages and restores fertility to natural cycles. From the Deva Flower Elixirs the Fig Tree essence offers an antidote to being overwhelmed by the complexity of the modern world, while the Findhorn Bell Heather brings tenacity and resilience to unwanted external changes.*

- If you are healing yourself, also put five drops of the dilute strength remedy dosage under your tongue.
- Light a single candle or lamp and sit in the semi-darkness.
- Play a tape of waves crashing, either one bought commercially or one you have taped yourself. Best of all sit on the seashore or within earshot of the sea.
- Focus on the point of light and move through it in your mind down a tunnel, deep into the ocean.
- In your mind's vision, enter a narrow cave surrounded by three huge stones. Pass through an abyss with a turning wheel of ice and a boiling cauldron. Feel the intense cold and then the steam. You are now in a green tent of nets under the sea, furnished with the skins of the finest sea animals. The Sea Mother has her back to you. Her hair and her aura are very tangled.
- Take a large comb, one made of a natural substance or a curved piece of shell, and gently comb the auric field around your own head. Hear the rhythmic swish of her falling hair as you symbolically comb out the shells that are tangled in the Sea Mother's beautiful tresses. As each tangle is overcome, so the energy will begin to flow and the blockages will be washed away by the sea. At this moment you will see hundreds of tiny iridescent rainbow fish swimming all around you, taking away any personal weakness or discomfort and filling the land with energy, light and new life. They are her gift in return for your help.
- Turn now and pass out of the tent, past the cauldron and the ice wheel and back through the tunnel, this time following a clear star at the other end as the tunnel becomes wider and wider until you are in the darkness again with only your small light.
- Blow out your candle and sit with only the sound of the sea, feeling the new life pulsating through yourself and the land.
- Do something to help the life to flow in a piece of land or coast near you, removing choking weeds from a stream or flower bed and perhaps joining a local campaign for purer water.

Chapter 9

PETS AND AURAS

Pets are more complex in their feeling and understanding than we give them credit for. Just as it is sometimes said only half-jokingly that we grow to resemble our pets – as with people who live together and have a strong emotional bond – we do become aurically linked with pets. Your animal may mirror you, especially your changing auric moods, so that your cat who sits motionless, close to you when you are sad or worried may be reflecting your own clouded green aura.

But because each creature does have a distinct personality – we can see this even in a tiny kitten or puppy – you can be uplifted by your cat's deep purple auric spirituality and by the permanently pink aura of love that all pets who are well cared for – and amazingly some who are not – develop towards their owners.

STUDYING THE AURA OF YOUR PET

Use the basic three circle auragram and study your pet at different times during the day and evening: in the early morning when you are both relaxed; when he or she displays excitement when you come home; when the animal reacts with hostility towards another creature; when she is in season and during sleep.

You will see the nature of your animal by their consistent auric colour, though if the pet is very angry, excited or frightened this may temporarily become flooded by the mood aura. You may find that your creature does display an aura that is surprising in view of its size or species and may explain why sometimes the animal *goes wild* or even acts destructively. Your aristocratic pooch's bright red aura suggests that it would benefit from days in the countryside where the innate mighty hunter instincts can be expressed chasing rabbits rather than savaging your shoes every time you leave them in the corner. The tiniest dogs can reveal leonine qualities in the aura and when you take time to reflect, he or she will often challenge a dog six or seven times their own size.

Cats tend to be a mysterious species – some say descended from the cat-headed Ancient Egyptian goddess Bast, protector of women, especially when pregnant and in childbirth. Many cats do display permanently indigo or deep purple auras, with often a touch of orange, indicating independence and desire for love on their terms. In contrast dogs tend to have a fair amount of green and pink, representing their utter unthinking devotion to you.

Horses may be golden brown, reliable, patient, trusting, though some stallions have the untamed auras of an ever-changing rainbow that if they only get to trot round a field can be manifest as behavioural fireworks. Domesticated birds may retain the blue of the sky, even if they only fly around the home, but if you see a lot of orange, then they may need to roam free for longer periods.

The following are auric meanings seen to be common among different animal species and can indicate when your animal needs a change in routine or extra care, especially if he or she has been especially comforting to you during a period of stress and so has become drained of energy.

White

As predominant permanent aura

You already know that your animal is very special, quite evolved, in fact a bit of a guardian angel. This creature will always instinctively soothe you when you are anxious or afraid. Incredibly telepathic, he or she will always know when you are coming home, even at unusual times and be waiting quietly by the door for you. You can talk to this creature about your deepest needs and will find that answers just come into your mind, always the right ones.

As a mood aura

Your pet is full of the life force right now, so go into the open air together – even a cat will luxuriate in extra sunlight. Do not be surprised if when you see this aura in a pet, unexpected but welcome contact from an absent friend or relative or someone new and exciting is imminent in your life – your pet's antennae are working overtime.

Red

As predominant permanent aura

A real fireball here, even if your pet is not much bigger than a hamster. This animal will need plenty of stimulation, activity – and maybe regular contact with the opposite sex of its species – if it is not to become bad-tempered or neurotic. Common in tom cats if not neutered.

As a mood aura

Maybe there has been a lot of tension in the household, or within you, and your animal is reacting to the general mood by displaying unusual restlessness. A little calm will do no harm, maybe a drop or two of soothing flower essence such as Chicory or Vine or the Five Flower Rescue Remedy, all commonly obtainable from the Bach Flower Remedy range, in the animal's water and in your own bath. My own favourite for hyperactive humans or pets is the Pacific Flower

Essence, Goatsbeard, that reduces tension in mind and body by creating an aura of calm to cope with stress situations.

Orange

As predominant permanent aura

This is the cat who walks alone or the dog who still hears the call of the wild even in an urban back yard. Let this creature come to you and direct you as to the way it should be cared for and you will know when your pet does snuggle close, it is by choice and out of pure love and not to obtain extra titbits.

As a mood aura

Maybe this pet has been petted once too often by children or the house has been particularly noisy. It is time for quality care and plenty of space – mental as well as physical.

Yellow

As predominant permanent aura

Who said animals were dumb? This is the creature who knows you are going out for the day while you're still in bed thinking about it – and will be lying against the door looking broken-hearted when you get up. This is the cat that catches the mouse and the dog who knows the way home even if you are lost in the middle of the woods.

As a mood aura

Not a usual aura for a pet. If he or she has been staying out a lot and refusing food, there may be a little old lady up the road trying to lure him away. So make sure that home comforts are of an extra high standard for a while.

Green

As predominant permanent aura

A very common colour in dogs and horses that are owned by one person and frequently petted. It is a colour that grows deeper and richer over the years. This pet would lay down his or her life for you.

The green of fish is paler and linked to their natural element water. But with Koi and other large fish the colour will deepen as you build a relationship.

As a mood aura

This will appear when you take a dog on a favourite walk, exercise your horse or stroke your cat – a common colour along with pink for contented creatures.

Blue

As predominant permanent aura

The colour of a wise friend, this pet would love you even if you could only afford the very cheapest food and will always have a calming effect on you, no matter how frantic or unfriendly the outside world. The natural colour of birds, this will become deeper as you talk to your bird and care for it.

As mood aura

A time just to be and not to do, to sit quietly in firelight or lamplight and communicate without words or even touch.

Purple

As predominant permanent aura

This is the aura of the old soul and as I have said, is often associated with felines. If you believe in reincarnation, then you may well have been with this creature in Ancient Egypt or Atlantis. But if that idea is too fanciful, this animal definitely has access to the collective wisdom of the universe, so in times of doubt, look deep into the creature's eyes and read the secrets that have perplexed humankind. If your pet is a cat, look through half-closed lids, as to stare is considered impolite in feline society.

As mood aura

Contemplative, this can indicate that you too should stop and wait and listen to the messages from the eternal sea of life rather than leaping in feet first. Imitate the cat and let your prey come to you.

Pink

As predominant permanent aura

Present to some degree in every creature, unless you obtain an animal from a rescue centre who has been ill-treated in the past. In this case it will take time and patience to restore. This is pure unconditional love and acceptance of what you are, but it will always return, for animals are incredibly forgiving of the frailties of the human race.

As mood aura

This tends to deepen in response to human needs. If you feel no one loves you or appreciates you, then your animal will exude pure acceptance. There are times when the company of your pet is preferable to anyone else in the world for this reason.

Brown

As predominant permanent aura

A colour of all earth creatures, this is aura of the faithful dog, the placid horse, rarely seen in cats, your animal will always be willing to go out with you rain or shine or stay in with you, even if spring is calling. It is the colour of man and woman's best friend and loyal follower.

As mood aura

Very calming if you are restless. Your animal will make no demands, but wait patiently until you are ready to rejoin the human race – and feed him or her. It is unusually slow as a mood aura to register change and for whole periods the brown mood aura may be virtually indistinguishable from the permanent aura.

Black

As predominant permanent aura

Seen in very old animals or sick ones who are losing the will to live or in rescued animals who will need a long period of calm and kindness for the darkness to lift. Seen also in animals who are grieving for an owner or mate.

As mood aura

Rarely experienced as animals are optimistic creatures. But dark streaks can indicate your pet needs healing before the illness reaches the physical level. It can sometimes indicate a chronic condition of which you are aware, but which may need more medical intervention to relieve the animal's exhaustion.

Grey

As predominant permanent aura

A creature of the night who roams alone and comes back with eyes sparkling. He or she is a guest in your home and if they choose to stay, then you are privileged. Also seen around reptiles and exotic pets who are out of their natural habitat.

As mood aura

Your animal is confused, which may result in withdrawn or destructive behaviour. Again grey streaks in the aura can indicate exhaustion or chronic stress or minor but persistent pain.

Silver

As predominant permanent aura

Rarely seen as this is a creature who is truly magical who may live and hunt by the cycles of the Moon and be happiest at night. Take seriously this pet's warnings of danger or dislikes of certain people and places.

As mood aura

This may indicate the presence of a ghost, which need not be frightening as it may be a former pet or loved relation. If the animal stares at a corner and wags it tail or purrs then all is well. Only if the animal becomes afraid or agitated should you bless the room by sprinkling it with salt dissolved in water and burn white candles and frankincense and sandal-wood oil to create a more benign atmosphere.

Gold

As predominant permanent aura

These are the creatures of legend, the animals who save lives or rescue lost children. If you have such a creature, you are very lucky as this colour is hardly ever seen in the auras of animals or people.

As mood aura

The colour of the peak experience when your horse is in full gallop with the wind teasing its mane or your dog is running through autumn leaves or along a sea shore. You may glimpse a moment of pure harmony and oneness with the universe – and if you are lucky you may pick up a little of the joy of the moment in your own aura.

HEALING PEOPLE WITH ANIMALS

The healing power and potential of animals, especially pets, is immense because of their open unconditional love and their loyalty and willingness to give without calculating reward or advantage. Recent research suggests that pet owners are healthier than non-pet owners, visiting doctors less frequently, having fewer colds and headaches, more regular heart rates, and lower cholesterol levels. It has been shown that the simple action of petting a dog can reduce blood pressure. It is also said that having a pet reduces your chance of having a heart attack, just as much as a low-salt diet or cutting down on alcohol.

This kind of research has led to the introduction of

schemes where animals are taken not only to visit their owners in hospital, but also other sick and depressed people, especially children and teenagers and older people in residential homes.

Of course you would not wish to drain your pet of energy but if you are sick or sad, then your pet's aura will often become especially green or pink or brown.

Exercise: Healing yourself using your pet

- *Stroke your pet a few centimetres away from his or her coat at the point where you feel the slight resistance to the auric field. Though you are not touching the fur, it will feel as though you are running your fingers through pure silk. Pets' auras are not huge and follow the contours of the body, but they are quite dense and so easily felt.*

- *Stroke the aura in circular movements, feeling the strength and love flowing from your pet's aura through your fingertips and circulating around your body. If you look quickly in a mirror after a few seconds you may see that you and your pet have virtually identical auras. A minute or two should be sufficient.*

- *Remember to feed your pet fresh, raw or lightly cooked rather than dried or canned food for the next meal and water that has been suffused in sunlight. If possible go out into the fresh air afterwards with the animal so that the natural life force can regenerate him or her.*

A HEALING RITUAL

If you notice that your animal's aura is dull or streaked with black or grey then he or she may need healing to prevent the exhaustion, stress or perhaps pollution from the atmosphere penetrating the physical body.

You can also supplement conventional veterinary or homoeopathic treatment with auric healing. Animals' auras are much easier to heal than human ones, except those of very small children, because your pets trust you entirely and do not try to rationalise the process.

If an animal is physically ill or has been hurt in an accident, then this ritual can be of great help to speed recovery. For chronic conditions you can repeat this ritual weekly. The ritual does not involve physical contact and so can give extra strength when your pet is resting or like human patients does not want to be touched.

Exercise: Healing your pet

- *Sit close to the animal or bird when he or she is asleep or totally relaxed.*

- *Create a circle of pure white or golden light around the animal's body, using a crystal pendulum, revolved nine times clockwise, set against the background of a fibre optic lamp or better still natural sunlight.*

- *Speak the animal's name several times very quietly, seeing the circle of light intensifying.*

- *Within the circle of light, visualise your pet in your mind's eye well and strong again and repeat the name this time silently, sending all your love as a green or pink ray – the healing colours for animals – to those places in the aura where you detected dark streaks of dullness or the parts of the body in which the illness or wound is manifest. For general illness or malaise, direct the colours all round the aura.*

- *For fever send blue and for conditions in which the animal has lost vitality, red or orange in addition to green and pink. See the light breaking into beams and cascading throughout the aura surrounding each paw and the tail right to the tips of the ears and the crown of the head.*

- *If your pet is in pain, hold the pendulum over the place of pain or the crown of the head and revolve it anti-clockwise, seeing a dark strand like wool leaving the aura. Then turn the pendulum nine times clockwise to infuse the aura with light and love.*

- *If the animal has to be in hospital or at a surgery for an operation or long-term treatment, you can carry out this ritual at the time of the treatment using a photograph or symbol.*

If your pet does die, it does not mean that your healing has failed; healing can mean a gentle parting if recovery would have left a beloved pet with a poor quality of life. In such a case, you may want to visualise the life force of the animal as a silver sphere rising upwards and away. Let the animal go as it came, with love and freely. Many people have told me that after death, they have still felt their pet's love and occasionally a brush of fur.

My own beloved very old white cat Haegl was becoming progressively sicker and more incontinent and on the day I finally decided she had reached the end of the road, she climbed voluntarily into the box I had lifted down to transport her. Normally she fought like a tiger in the veterinary surgeon's office. But this time she sat quietly in the box, motionless on the vet's table and when she had the final injection, sank into sleep with a sigh of relief. I noticed that during the day her aura was getting paler, as though she was letting go of life. Sometimes, as in the case of Haegl, auric healing can effect a peaceful passing.

Chapter 10

DEVELOPING YOUR AURA WORK PERSONALLY AND PROFESSIONALLY

Some people use their evolving psychic gifts in interpreting auras within their circle of family and friends to offer wise counsel, to give strength in times of crisis, to heal sorrows and help trigger innate self-healing energies. But an increasing number of people are recognising that because aura reading is a very accurate and sensitive form of divination, it is a powerful tool for counselling and healing work in the wider sphere.

Through interpreting changes in an aura, over a number of sessions, you can guide people through a process of increasing self-awareness of their inner thoughts and feelings. What is more, unlike conventional divinatory readings, aura work provides gentle positive therapy within the counselling session itself. For as well as detecting areas of potential change or challenge for a client through aura interpretation, you can work on cleansing, balancing, strengthening and healing the aura and above all showing the client how he or she can protect and empower the aura themselves. Thus it is a very proactive form of counselling.

If you are relatively new to aura work, it may be helpful to gain experience by giving aura readings to friends, acquaintances and the remarkable number of 'acquaintances of acquaintances' who will seemingly by telepathic means find their way to your door or your corner at work or at a party with the inevitable, 'What can you see in my aura then?'

When you feel confident, you may decide to begin to accept payment for your work. Some people feel that anything to do with healing should not involve monetary transactions, although 'paying the shaman' is considered a vital part of healing among indigenous tribes, what is more, as with any other skill, whether you are reupholstering antique furniture, counselling by more conventional methods or planning a makeover of someone's wardrobe or the decor of their home, you are justified in charging for your time and expertise.

At first, you may be more comfortable accepting gifts or donations for charity – and indeed a charity function or a healing festival often provides an excellent way to discover if you do wish to earn a living this way, as you have to cope with a number of clients over a relatively short period. If you do decide to turn professional, you can visit people in their homes or set aside an area of your own home to receive visitors. The best readers rarely advertise and work on recommendation which in itself gives you some protection from less desirable visitors who may seek to exploit you. But even if you do not work professionally, you can adapt the ideas of this chapter to your informal counselling work.

In practice a high proportion of aura readers combine interpretation with healing and balancing and a degree of teaching as you show clients how they can continue the work at home between visits. You may find that a point comes when you do want to take a course in healing, especially if you encounter people with chronic or more serious physical and mental conditions. The only danger comes when aura practitioners do fail to emphasise that aura work is one aspect of wellbeing and healing but that a physically or emotionally sick person must obtain conventional medical care or consult a recognised alternative practitioner.

However, you can use aura divination, as you would Tarot

cards or runes; to identify areas of difficulty and opportunities that have not yet been utilised or potential as yet undeveloped. In this case, follow the stages listed below as far as seems relevant and spend time at the end of a session, discussing practical ways of implementing the desired changes. Regular follow-up visits can be helpful, as even minor improvements in lifestyle or attitude will be reflected in a clearer, brighter aura.

PREPARING FOR COUNSELLING AND HEALING THE AURA

Whether you are working with your family and friends or setting up in practice, it can be helpful to gather together all the materials you will need in one place.

If you do work away from home, for example at a healing festival, you will need a large, well-supported bag or case so that diagrams do not become crumpled or paints scattered. It is a good grounding exercise as well to mark the end of the session for yourself and your client, if you clear and pack everything away, while returning conversation to the everyday sphere.

The simplest equipment often works better than elaborate or expensive tools and if you have any spare money, it is better to spend it on good quality oils, paints and crystals rather than, for example, a massage couch. A sofa or a pile or cushions at home or a comfortable chair at a festival are just as effective and more relaxing. You will also need:

- *A set of paints or crayons in a variety of shades with which to colour your auragrams and you can also use these with your pendulum to instantly assess the auric colours, if you are finding any area problematic (see page 45).*

- *A crystal pendulum to use for identifying auric colours either as above, directly or from a colour chart. Your pendulum can also identify blockages if held over the head and used to remove these and then to restore energy and light (page 47).*

- *Your colour chart mounted on stiff card and laminated ready to supplement your clairvoyant vision.*

- *A series of auragrams, both the three circle kind (pages 61–2) for quick readings and the full nine circle auragram (pages 88–9 and 95) for longer sessions. The less detailed auragram is good to use when you meet a person for the first time, to gain an initial impression to begin the session. Clear plastic wallets with sticky labels for names are useful both for you and clients to keep previous auragrams in for comparison.*

- *A variety of coloured candles and crystals for cleansing, balancing and healing work as different clients may seem to prefer certain materials (see chapters 7 and 8).*

- *A bag with a set of crystals in different shades is another useful tool for identifying auric colours quickly (see pages 44–7 and 76).*

- *Incenses or oils to represent the different levels of the aura (page 94) also cedar, sage and sweetgrass or the alternatives listed on pages 105–6 – for smudging to cleanse the aura.*

BEGINNING THE SESSION

Remember to protect your own aura before you begin, so that you do not become exhausted by what is a very intense form of assessment and therapy on the practitioner as well as the client (see page 100 for the gentle pink shield of harmony). An hour is long enough to develop a rapport and work on the aura longer and you will become tired and the benefits to the client begin to decrease.

Exercise: Giving a professional aura reading

Make hand contact to establish an initial auric impression (see page 52), then look at the aura either externally or using your inner clairvoyant vision, softly speaking words of greeting while you do so to keep the psychic rapport flowing. If the aura seems blurred or your sense the person is unconsciously trying to mask the aura, use one of the less direct methods, such as the pendulum on a colour chart.

At each stage explain what you are doing and talk about the colours of the aura generally. Then ask if there are any specific areas of concern or feelings of tiredness or pain. As you listen, allow your hand to select colours and colour the first basic auragram. When this is done, you can make a first tentative assessment, explaining the meanings of the colours/shades (see chapter 3) in relation to the client's current world and asking for the person's own input.

Mention any areas of darkness, jaggedness and holes or tears that are manifest in the basic auragram, but keep this very positive as people can become very worried if they think they may become ill. If someone has already mentioned an area of discomfort, then it can be useful to discuss the problem in terms of stress and explore practical steps to reduce work-load or resolve family problems. In this way, difficulties are seen as challenges leading to beneficial changes.

You can, with the agreement of your client, suggest that you perhaps cleanse and restore energy or balance to the whole aura. This will usually have fairly rapid beneficial effects – you may need to build up a rapport over several sessions before you begin more focused healing work. Smudging is an excellent preliminary cleansing method already mentioned. Then you can use colour breathing to restore balance to the aura (see pages 107–9).

You may like to light candles in the colours your client needs to inhale or give them crystals in the appropriate colours as a focus. This is especially helpful if the person is new to psychic work.

As you work with your subject, stop before each new colour pairing and at each stage ask him or her to visualise their exhaled breath in the colour you describe and to inhale the appropriate candle/crystal colour. Take your time in this stage, so you can teach your client how they can work between sessions before you as you work with the patient. At the same time you are drawing darker, duller colours from their aura and replacing them from the candle/crystal colours as you direct the energies towards the other aura.

Finally you need to seal or protect the aura and then show the client how to strengthen his or her own aura using one of the techniques described on pages 75–80. Do another very quick auragram to show the patient the after-effects of even a short cleansing session and with the client, plan how they can make immediate plans to reduce stress levels and maximise opportunities. Then you need to slow down the energies and close the session for both of you. If you did not light a candle in the colour visualisation, light a gentle pink or purple one now and extinguish all other lights. Sit facing your client with the candle between you for two or three minutes in silence, allowing the light to permeate both your auras.

Finally suggest you blow out the candle together, sending the light to loved ones and above all to the self, letting flow into the darkness any remaining doubts or resentments. Perhaps have a cup of tea together and as you tidy away your things, you can return the talk to general matters and the session draws naturally to a close.

When he or she has gone, either sprinkle sacred water over your aura or, if it is evening, add nine drops to your bath and cleanse your chakras, using the exercise I suggested on pages 103–4. You can, if you have a photocopier, give the client a copy of the auragrams or alternatively post a copy to the subject when you have scanned it in to the computer or drawn it.

SUBSEQUENT SESSIONS

These should again last no more than an hour. Protect your own aura before you begin. This time after your initial hand contact, you can ask your client for an update on his or her life and health while you create a more complex auragram. Though it has more circles, the auragram is no more complex than the three circle model.

Exercise: Giving a subsequent aura reading

- *As before, fill in the central circles first with the predominant permanent and then the mood aura.*

- *Then let your mind's vision (or maybe external vision if this is how you see auras) cast a pure white aura around the subject, which will then – if you wait and let your client continue to talk – divide into the seven auric layers.*

- *You can use your pendulum and colour chart to help you, if your clairvoyant eye becomes bogged down by conscious thought or expectations – remember the actual colours may run counter to what the client is saying. In practice the outer two layers are rarely seen or only very faintly. If a layer is missing, it may be that the level below has suffused it with colour or that this is an area that is very weak and needs work.*

- *Mark any bulges or missing areas and any dark streaks, jagged lines or tears.*

- *Place the finished diagram between you and explain very simply the significance of the different levels in relation to what is recorded.*

- *Compare the colours of the predominant aura and the mood aura with the before and after diagrams of the previous session and note at which levels these colours are predominant in the new more detailed auragram.*

- *Go through the information slowly, allowing the client to ask questions and to make input. This may take some time and this talk can be as important to helping the client as the healing or cleansing – indeed sensitive words can be the most effective healing method of all.*

- *You may wish to light incense or essential oil in the fragrance linked to any auric layers that especially seem to need attention (page 94) or use a Crown chakra incense, for example frankincense or sandalwood, to permeate the whole system. The advantage of using oils rather than incense is that you can add two or three fragrances to the same burner.*

- *As before cleanse and balance the aura.*

However, you may decide with the client to begin basic healing work, emphasising that the key lies in self-healing. Before you can start, explain the stages that you will carry out and afterwards demonstrate any techniques that will be helpful to the subject at home or at work.

- *Using the auragram, go through the stages listed in Chapter 8 and finally seal the aura with gentle protection.*
- *Draw only a simple auragram to end the session. This will reflect clearer, brighter, but less harsh, colours. The healing of the different levels may need several sessions and time to register as changes within the individual layers – the benefits will be seen when you draw an auragram at the beginning of the next session.*
- *Make plans for your client's self-healing and aura strengthening work between sessions and talk about any difficulties they experienced putting into practice the techniques you introduced during the previous session – usually it is just a question of suggesting a different approach or perseverance.*
- *Bring the session to a gentle conclusion as before. You may need to untangle your own aura, if there was a lot of negativity in the client's aura.*

It is difficult to assess how many sessions will be needed, but initially at least a weekly interval should occur to allow the work to take effect. As the effects of self-healing kick in, so sessions can be reduced to fortnightly or even monthly and thereafter a client may visit only major change points once or twice a year. That is a real sign you have succeeded.

Some people with difficult lives or chronic conditions may continue to need a number of sessions, perhaps with a few weeks in between. If you encounter a really difficult person who insists his or her life is perfect, relationships are wonderful and career is fulfilling, you may wonder why he or she has come at all – only to notice an incredibly harsh or cloudy aura.

You may need to begin with cleansing and untangling before you can start to approach the problems – usually these people turn out to be really responsive subjects once they have shed their initial barriers.

Aura readings and relationships

You can work with two emotionally connected people – family members, lovers, partners or close friends – who want to improve or resolve temporary difficulties in their relationships.

This can be a minefield for an outsider, so before you begin protect yourself with a very strong pink shield and ensure your own aura is untangled before you begin. You may need up to an hour and a half to work separately and together with the pair. But because this work is draining, you would probably not want to undertake more than two or three sessions a day.

Working with two people on relationship issues

With joint sessions, you need a separate area in which one person can read, play music, relax while the other raises any private concerns about the relationship and you work on cleansing and strengthening the individual auras. A very unified couple may want to be present while the other's aura is being cleansed, especially if there is a lot of untangling to be done, but on the whole this does not work well.

You can however spend time at the end of the session suggesting joint auric strengthening exercises to be carried out at home. These tend to have positive effects on all areas of a relationship and after two or three sessions you can introduce any necessary healing work on the relationship – couples tend to be very skilled at healing each other, as discussed in chapter 5.

You will need to be incredibly tactful when working with

couples. For example if one of the partners is, or is contemplating, being unfaithful – a scarlet aura with neon rays directed beyond the partner (page 67) could indicate this. However, it is not your place to reveal that you have discovered psychically – either to the person or the partner. Equally, if you see that one partner is dominating or draining the other emotionally you have to be careful to cast the situation in a very positive light and study both auras carefully to see whether the victim is entirely unaware or is colluding in some way.

The easiest method to allow the couple to draw their own conclusions is to draw two simple auragrams on a large sheet of paper with space between them on which to make interconnecting areas and rays passing either one way or in both directions. For relationship auragrams two outlines of the human body can help to identify connections of the heart as rays pass from one to the other. You can then draw the circles round the bodies and mark the rays between the two. You may notice auras that the auragrams mirror each other if the couple are emotionally close, are united in a joint venture/problem or have lived together for many years.

Because you are dealing with two people initial hand contact may not give you a differentiated picture of the separate auras so you may wish to use one of the instant methods on pages 50–55. Even after the first session, a new auragram will often reveal clearer and less tangled auric connections.

Relationship readings are generally focused towards emotional issues, so if one partner does complain of feeling exhausted or unwell, he or she may benefit from an individual session on another day when their whole life, as well as relationship issues, can be assessed and healing given.

Julia and Richard – a case study

Julia and Richard came to me after I met them at a healing festival, because they were uncertain about whether they should get married as soon as they left university and take up jobs in the same town. Their relationship had been quite sudden and very intense until the last month when they had planned to pursue their separate careers. Julia had been offered postgraduate training in France, while Richard was due to take up a position with a legal firm in his home town in the North of England to work towards attaining his charter, a post that would involve study in the evening and several residential courses in London at weekends.

As they stood side by side, they were joined at the head, Richard's bright clear yellow and Julia's a rich green. Only from Julia came a green beam from her heart to Richard's indicating that her life and emotions were far more entangled with Richard's than his were with hers.

Using a pendulum over a colour chart, I confirmed what I *saw*, that Julia's predominant permanent aura was also pure rich green, indicating that her love for Richard was colouring her world and directing her priorities towards their relationship, suggesting she might be considering abandoning her trip to France, although she had not told Richard this.

Her current mood aura was dull or dirty orange, indicating that Julia was feeling possessive, maybe because she subconsciously detected uncertainty in the relationship on Richard's part.

The third circle, for subsidiary colours in the simple aura-gram, showed a much murkier green, indicating perhaps that resentment and doubts were beginning to cloud her love, although she could not pinpoint a reason, as Richard was externally as loving as before.

In contrast Richard's permanent aura and mood aura were both a clear yellow, indicating that his mind was firmly set on his future career. There was a pale green as the tertiary colour, so obviously he did love Julia still. It was just that his emotions were not currently centre stage.

So this was difficult: as I did not want to fuel Julia's insecurity further, nor was it fair to work on Richard's aura to strengthen his love if it was not what he wanted. So we talked about the different meanings and Julia admitted she was prepared to sacrifice all for love, which was not a problem for Richard who said she would easily find a teaching job in his home town. However, Julia was making a sacrifice for a guy who did not feel as strongly as she did.

So the crucial aura to work with was Julia's, to strengthen her own identity, so that if she decided to go with Richard, it was for the right reasons. When we were alone, I cleared her aura of a number of tangles that had shown as murky streaks and which were, I suspected, unreturned love that was slowly turning sour.

There were no holes, but using candles and colour breathing, I helped her to add a clear indigo to offer the necessary detachment to restore the balance in the relationship and gave her an orange amber crystal in her power hand (the one she wrote with) to strengthen her own identity. I also added a little pink to her aura by placing a rose quartz crystal in her other hand to allay her deep-seated anxieties that, however justifiable, were preventing her from seeing the situation clearly.

For Richard, I made the yellow even clearer and richer – his aura was free from tangles or holes, so that the communicative quality of yellow would come to the fore and he could reassure Julia that his preoccupation with his own career was only a temporary focus and that he did still love her. On the other hand, if he was no longer deeply in love, he needed to deal with this in the light of the promises he had made to her only weeks before, that he would follow her to the ends of the earth if necessary.

I also gave him deep altruistic blue, in the form of a sodalite crystal to hold in his power hand so that his ambitions were softened by a sense of responsibility towards Julia. For if she did give up her plans to travel, then she needed at least some assurance of a long-term commitment.

Back together, I tactfully suggested that love could grow

stronger with partings and regular meetings and that Julia should not necessarily dismiss going to France while Richard was busy establishing himself on the career ladder.

The final auragram surprisingly showed that already the murky green in Julia's third circle was becoming brighter and clearer and that indigo and orange were seeping into her mood aura. Richard's outer green aura was becoming deeper and for the first time beams were moving from him, albeit slowly, toward Julia's heart. He said that he suddenly realised that he was taking Julia for granted and that he was being unfair and the yellow actually softened to become more of a buttercup yellow, indicative of family life.

I suggested that Richard and Julia continued the candle and crystal work at home and also that they burned green and blue candles to maintain loving energies between them in a time of change. By the time they returned two weeks later their auras were much more in harmony, with Julia's ambitions rekindled as Richard's love was reactivated.

Julia decided to go abroad. It was Richard who visited France whenever he was free and the last I heard they were planning a future together.

Working with one person on relationship issues

However usually only one person comes to the session and he or she may be experiencing a difficult work or home situation. Sometimes a lover or partner has deserted them (or occasionally died), but the influence of this person is still having a profound effect on the aura. In the case of a desertion your client may be confused, wanting the person back but at the same time feeling angry and wounded at the betrayal. This is quite intense and can release a lot of free-floating hostility, so cleanse your own aura before beginning and protect it with a shield of silver and gold (see pages 98–9). Such cases are often like a jigsaw puzzle with missing pieces, but such work can be immensely rewarding.

As with a relationship session in which both parties are present, you can see rays entering and leaving the aura of the person you are studying. If you ask your client to talk about the relationship that is causing problems, you will be able to identify by the colour and intensity of the rays created what is going on.

More positively during the session or perhaps over a series, you can help the client to rid themselves of negative or emotionally draining pressures from the absent source of tension or sorrow.

Begin the session with hand contact and a simple three circle auragram again, but this time do not colour it until you have talked to your subject about the relationship, as this is the focus of the session.

Exercise: Relationship healing with an absent partner

- *Draw two auragrams with a space between, but this time leave the second circle blank, for now use just the circle shapes and not the human outlines.*

- *Concentrate on the rays entering and leaving the aura while the subject recalls the person causing the strong emotions, which need not necessarily be hostile – indeed there may be ambivalence.*

- *Now concentrate on the absent person's aura. More permanent feelings coming from the predominant aura tend to be stronger and matt in colour, while those from the mood aura will be less stable and may contain lights or streaks. So you can create an approximation of the other half of the relationship and more importantly can see the bi-directional lines, which may be at odds with what the subject is saying and thinks he or she means. Another person's effect on us is not only when we think or speak to them, but when we recall them by thinking or speaking of them. In fact, speaking about the person will often elicit vibes almost as strong as if the person was present.*

145

- *Even if the person causing the pain died years earlier, the imprints of the aura as it impinged on the person during lifetime may still be tangled in the client's own aura. So you may need to unravel a very tangled aura and then work over several sessions clearing away, cleansing, repairing and finally sealing the aura to enable your client to be truly free.*

- *If a relationship issue is complex or old wounds are deep explain to your subject that he or she must not be discouraged if results seem slow. It may be that conventional counselling and practical help from other agencies are needed if a current relationship is abusive or there are related problems (eg financial worries).*

- *Smudging is a very potent method of cleansing in the initial session and the person may like to burn the smudging herbs as oils or incense regularly at home.*

AURA READING AND PAST LIFE WORK

If a present dilemma is proving resistant to auric cleansing and healing, it may be helpful to explore memories of a past world that may be contained within the aura. There is much disagreement as to the way that the past affects our aura. Since we carry within ourselves the genes of our distant ancestors, it would be surprising if this connection with past worlds was not reflected in the aura.

One interpretation of such memories is that we spontaneously recollect or create relevant past life scenarios as we make connection with a collective source of wisdom, accessed by the connection of our personal aura with a cosmic one. This past life is a symbolic way of understanding and resolving present dilemmas, especially in cases where for example a fear of flying or confined places is both resistant to conventional therapies and the subject cannot find a cause in early life that may have triggered the phobia. Whether this is a psychological or psychic process, past life recall is usually helpful and one way of accessing these *memories* or *symbols* is through the aura.

However, there is growing evidence that reincarnation, the belief that our soul returns to a new body after death, may have a valid basis. Dr Ian Stevenson is Head of the Department of Psychiatric Medicine at the University of Virginia and has studied reincarnation for more than thirty years. Dr Stevenson found that young children gave the most consistent results in past life recollection of all the subjects he tested, but that they lost spontaneous recall of earlier worlds at around the age of seven.

Perhaps the most significant evidence for reincarnation in Stevenson's research is his finding that 35 per cent of the 895 children who claimed to remember previous lives, possessed either birthmarks of an unusual kind or had birth defects, not linked to any apparent genetic or physiological cause. These birth scars correlated with wounds apparently inflicted on the person whose life the child recalled as his or her own in an earlier existence, some of which were verified on medical records of the deceased.

It has been hypothesised that memories of these past lives, if such they are, would reside within the *etheric* or spirit body that exists within the physical body and may be the essential self that survives death. There is disagreement at which level these memories would be manifest, but the question is largely philosophical, since all parts of the etheric self are inter-related and are contained within the auric field.

If a subject can be relaxed into a light trance state, akin to a meditative state, then an aura reader will see the aura change, sometimes quite dramatically, and a particularly strong aura from what may be a past life will appear. At this point the subject will, if questioned, recount experiences apparently from a past world and may use a different vocabulary or speech patterns.

In Chapter 4 on Interpreting Auras, I mentioned the flash-bulb technique as a common psychological phenomenon whereby memories about a particularly dramatic event were captured intact. One theory would be that a particular aura state associated with a dramatic event in a past world was captured within the person's deep memory, to be reactivated in the relaxed state.

If you want to practise this technique personally to work on your own aura, you will need a friend or family member who is confident about auras to identify the changes in the aura, to help you to relax and to offer gentle, objective questioning aura colour...

Exercise: Working with past lives as part of a counselling session

- *Cleanse your own aura before the session.*
- *Cleanse your subject's aura of negativity. This will not remove the past life memories or interfere with the past life symbolism, but will prevent any negative emotions interfering with the process or causing distress.*
- *Draw the auragram as it is after cleansing using the three circles, but do not discuss it with the subject at this stage.*
- *Ask the subject to sit or lie quietly and breathe slowly and deeply through the nose, holding the breath for three seconds and then breathing out slowly through the mouth.*
- *You can breathe and count with them, taking care you do not send yourself into too relaxed a state.*
- *Using a slow, monotonous, gentle tone begin by creating the entry point into a past world. There is a variety of scenes you can evoke on which your subject can be transported, a magic carpet flying through the night sky, a boat floating down a stream, a carousel that spins into a different world, a flight of steps, a misty road that turns a sudden corner and when the mist clears the scene has changed. You can create your own scenes as though you were telling a fairy story, tales that have their roots in ancient mythology.*
- *If your client is comfortable with the idea, you can tape the session so that you can match details to the auragrams.*
- *Once you have transported your client to this other world,*

you will need an actual entry point – a doorway, a tunnel towards a point of light, a waterfall, a rainbow curtain.

- *Incorporate a process counting either from 1–10 or if you prefer a slower entry reciting the alphabet, so that you can lead your client to the new dimension gradually and later back into the everyday world by reversing the order.*

- *Say something like, 'You are standing at the top of a flight of nine steps. The sun is warm. As you walk down them you cease to be aware of your body and what is going on all around you. 1, 2, 3 – the sun dazzles your vision and you can no longer see the room you have left – 4, 5, 6 – now you can only hear the gentle birdsong, the humming of the bees – 7, 8, 9 – you are getting lighter and your feet are almost floating – 10 and you step on to a carpet of flowers. Walk across the soft, fragrant carpet until you see a building with a door – open the door and if you wish you can go inside –'.*

- *You should now see the aura, especially the mood aura changing – you may need to create several basic auragrams during the experience.*

- *Ask your subject to describe the scene. You can add questions – but not leading ones – about the clothes he or she is wearing, other people who are present and the surroundings.*

- *At any potentially worrying point repeat, 'You are only observing the scene, watching the person you once were and you can return to the everyday world at any time. Nothing can harm you.'*

- *When your subject has reached the end of the scenario reverse the order, taking him or her back along the road and up the steps or along the road or stream to your entry point, this time counting back from 10–1 or Z–A very slowly.*

- *At the visualised steps say something like, 'As you climb each step you will begin to wake. 10, 9, 8 – you can hear the sounds of the everyday world, 7, 6, 5 – you can feel your body beginning to move – 4, 3, 2 – you can see all around you quite clearly and – 1 – you wake refreshed and renewed'.*

- *The aura will be changed by the experience. Sometimes these changes occur in the more permanent colour. This is a very promising sign as it usually means that the client has left some trauma or unresolved matter behind.*

- *Show your client the changing auragrams and allow him or her to talk about the experience and to draw parallels between the past world experience and current issues.*

- *Afterwards cleanse the aura as if it has been on a journey, removing any tangles left by the experience. Seal the aura with a gentle pink, before gradually bringing the session to a close.*

CONCLUSION –
THE RAINBOW OF LIFE

Auras are an integral part of ourselves, the mirror of our mind, body and soul. They are the point at which our unique energies interact with those of other people, the natural world and the cosmos itself. They link us with the earth and also with the stars. Yet auras are not the preserve of experts or of those who try to constrict what is essentially a constantly evolving spiritual phenomenon into precise rays of light to be measured and analysed. Settling on one definition of the aura and how to interpret auric energies is like trying to capture the life force by putting a stopper in an empty bottle.

The greatest experts on auras are children who take them for granted, as they do all the wondrous dimensions through which they pass as effortlessly as walking through a shaft of sunlight. If you want to truly understand auras, put down the cameras and other devices for measuring a fraction of the brilliance. Go instead for a walk with a young child and ask him or her to point out the colours they see. If you can momentarily suspend rational thoughts, you can glimpse through their eyes the wonderful Technicolor world that radiates from all creation.

As we live and move and laugh and cry, so our auras form an ever-changing rainbow and the more we give to the world, the more extensive and radiant our own aura becomes.

Whether you are a beginner or have worked with auras for

many years, this book provides an introduction to your own ongoing explorations of auras in the world around. The more you work with the auras of nature as well as people, and the less you consciously try to ascribe logical significance to your perceptions, the more naturally your intuitive awareness will flow and with it your ability to heal the aura through your own auric energies.

As I write this, it is a grey afternoon and I have many worries about my young son Bill whose vision of the world makes it hard for him to be educated within the existing educational system. I am fretting about deadlines and unpaid bills and as I glance in the mirror my aura is grey, tired and lifeless. But then my daughter Miranda comes in from school glowing golden with life and excitement as she gets ready to go dancing, and green, perhaps with the stirrings of a first romance. My son Jack is unusually reflective, his aura with deep blue as he finishes his examinations and his childhood and moves into the world of work.

My tame blackbird sings at the door, his aura silver as he flutters and hops. The flowers on my tiny terrace are red and pink and purple and as I water them their fragrance fills me with colour. Then Bill phones from his boarding school, excited about coming home and riding his bicycle around the caravan site where we spend weekends. He is pleased because he has been playing in the woods with his classmates without problems. I can sense the orange as his self-esteem rises and he strives to be independent of me which he soon must be.

And so, by the time I return to writing this, having cleared away the dishes and fed the hedgehog who has come trundling up in the twilight for his food, my aura is quite bright and much clearer. I can see the rich golden brown I borrowed from the hedgehog as he banged his empty bowl for food and did not run away when I filled it. I have Miranda's green and gold, Jack's blue, the purple of my favourite flowers, the soaring silver of the bird that is still singing in the tree outside. The Moon is almost full and so I will draw strength from that too. And another day when I am confident and full of vitality, I will share my auric colours with someone who is sad or worried or just tired.

For that is the key to auras and all the exercises and the interpretations are just ways, valuable ways, of trying to understand this quite spontaneous and yet wondrous gift we all possess, swirling around us, drawing and giving strength. We are our auras and they are us.

It is said the aura of Buddha extended several miles, which is certainly not a fanciful concept. For our spiritual energies are not finite, but expand and extend as we grow and enrich our understanding of ourselves and the world around us. Maybe the future of the universe depends on our collective aura and so in this way we can each one of us make our mark on eternity.

FURTHER READING

AURAS

Andrews, Ted, *How to See and Read the Aura*, Llewellyn, 1994

Brennan, Barbara Ann, *Hands of Light: a Guide to Healing through the Human Energy Field*, Bantam, 1987

Lindgren, C.E., *Capturing the Aura: Integrating Science, Technology and Metaphysics*, Blue Dolphin Press, 2000

Roberts, Ursula, *Look at the Aura – and Learn*, Greater World Association, 1975

Van Gelder Kunz, Dora, *The Personal Aura*, Theosophical Publishing House, 1991

CHAKRAS

Choquette, Sonia, *Balancing Your Chakras*, Piatkus Books, 2000

Dale, Cyndi, *New Chakra Healing, The Revolutionary 32-Center Energy System*, Llewellyn, 1996

Karagulla, Shafica and Van Gelder Kunz, Dora, *Chakras and the Human Energy Field*, Theosophical University Press, 1994

White, Ruth, *Chakras*, Piatkus Books, 1998

COLOUR HEALING

Buckland, Ray, *Practical Color Magic*, Llewellyn, 1995

Klotsche, Charles, *Color Medicine: The Secrets of Color/ Vibrational Healing*, Light Technology Publications, 1993
McLeod, June, *Colours of the Soul*, Piatkus Books, 2000
Sun, Howard and Dorothy, *Colour Your Life*, Piatkus, 1999
Wills, Pauline, *Colour Healing Manual*, Piatkus Books, 2000

CRYSTALS

Bourgault, Luc, *The American Indian Secrets of Crystal Healing*, Quantum, 1997
Cunningham, Scott, *Encyclopaedia of Crystal, Gem and Metal Magic*, Llewellyn, 1991
Holbeche, Soozi, *The Power of Gems and Crystals*, Piatkus Books, 1990

FLOWER REMEDIES

Barnard, Julian, *A Guide to the Bach Flower Remedies*, C. W. Daniel Co., 1992
Harvey, Clare G. and Cochrane, Amanda, *The Encyclopaedia of Flower Remedies*, Thorsons/HarperCollins, 1995
Korte, Andreas, *Orchids, Gemstones and the Healing Energies*, Bauer Berlag, 1993
Wildwood, Chrissie, *The Encyclopedia of Healing Plants*, Piatkus Books, 1999

INCENSES AND OILS

Cunningham, Scott, *Complete Book of Oils, Incenses and Brews*, Llewellyn, 1991
Dunwich, Gerena, *Wicca Garden, a Witch's Guide to Magical and Enchanted Herbs and Plants*, Citadel, 1996

KIRLIAN POTOGRAPHY/BIOFIELDS

Acupuncture and Western Hemisphere Conference on Kirlian

Photography, *The Energies of Consciousness in Acupuncture, Auras and Kirlian Photography*, Gordon and Breach Science Publications, 1975

Useful Addresses

Meditation/visualisation music

UK

Beechwood Music
Littleton House
Littleton Road
Ashford
Middlesex
TW15 1UU

Australia

New World Productions
PO Box 244 WBO
Red Hill
Queensland 4059

US

Raven Recordings
744 Broad Street
Room 1815
Newark
New Jersey 07102

SPIRITUAL HEALING ORGANISATIONS

UK

British Alliance of Healing Associations
c/o Mrs Jo Wallace
3 Sandy Lane
Gisleham
Lowestoft
Suffolk
NR33 8EQ

Tel: 01502 742224

National Federation of Spiritual Healers
Old Manor Farm Studio
Church Street
Sunbury on Thames
Middlesex
TW16 6RG

Tel: 01932 783164
Email: office@nfsh.org.uk
Website: www.nfsh.org.uk

Australia

Australian Spiritualist Association
PO Box 248
Canterbury
New South Wales 2193

Canada

National Federation of Spiritual Healers (Canada)
Call for information: +1 416 284 4798

Spiritualist Church of Canada
1835 Lawrence Ave East
Scarborough
Ontario
M1R 2Y3

US

World Light Center
PO Box 425
Wappingers Falls
NY 12590
USA

Tel: +1 914 297 2867
Email: worldlight@worldlightcenter.com
Website: www.worldlightcenter.com

INDEX

PIATKUS BOOKS

If you have enjoyed reading this book, you may be interested in other titles published by Piatkus. These include: